PLAY TENNIS WITH ROSEWALL

PLAY TENNIS
WITH ROSEWALL

BY
KEN ROSEWALL

IN COLLABORATION WITH
JOHN BARRETT

PUBLISHED BY
QUEEN ANNE PRESS LTD

© John Barrett/Ken Rosewall 1975

House Editor Peter Dunk
Cover photo courtesy of Colorsport

Design and Instructional diagrams by David Fordham
Illustrations on pp 48-51 by Andrew Farmer

Written by Ken Rosewall in collaboration with John Barrett, editor of the BP/Commercial Union *World of Tennis* Yearbook (Queen Anne Press) in which much of this material has previously appeared.

All rights reserved. This book is sold subject to the condition that it shall not, by way of trade or otherwise, be lent, re-sold, hired out, or otherwise circulated without the publisher's prior consent in any form of binding or cover other than that in which it is published and without a similar condition including this condition being imposed on the subsequent purchaser. No part of this publication may be reproduced, stored in a retrieval system or transmitted in any form or by any means whatsoever, photocopied, recorded or otherwise without the prior permission of the publisher.

Filmset in Monophoto Souvenir by C. E. Dawkins (Typesetters) Ltd., Southwark, London.
Printed in England by Fletcher & Son, Norwich.

Published by Queen Anne Press Limited 12 Vandy Street London EC2A 2EN.

CONTENTS

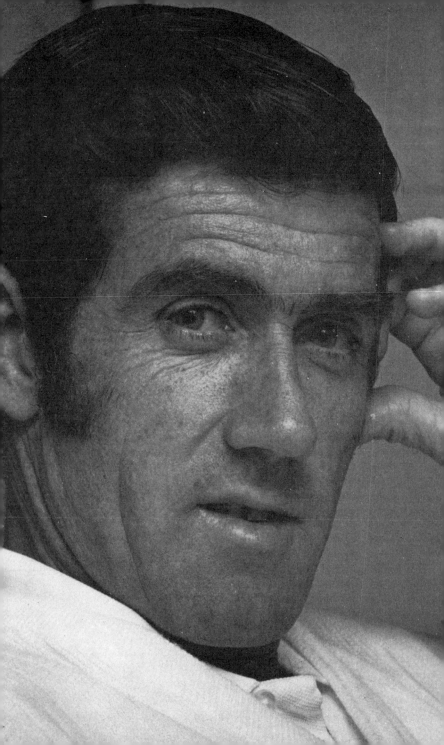

For my wife Wilma
whose ready acceptance of a difficult role has made it possible
for me to pursue my career long after less fortunate men have
retired from the game. And for my sons Brett and Glen
who, at times, must have wondered if they had a father.

AN APPRECIATION
by Dan Maskell OBE

Dan Maskell who has seen every Wimbledon since 1924, was the All England professional from 1928-55; the Training Manager to the LTA from 1955-73 and has covered Wimbledon for BBC TV every year since 1950.

In all the years that I have been watching tennis I cannot think of a single player who has embodied all the finest qualities of skill and sportsmanship, style and chivalry, in greater measure than Ken Rosewall.

Technically Ken has brought me immense pleasure with his flawless groundstrokes (shall we ever see a more graceful or more penetrating backhand?), his rapier-like volleys, his immaculate footwork, and effortless court coverage. But it has always remained a paradox for me that a man with a relatively weak serve – his only blemish – should have possessed such a decisive and powerful smash. Above all, Ken, like that great French artist Henri Cochet, has proved that you do not have to be a giant of 6 ft 4 in., weigh 200 lb, and wield the racket like a toothpick to succeed. If the quality of genius is there, as it certainly has been with him, size is unimportant.

The really astonishing thing about Ken Rosewall–the quality that sets him apart from the rest – is endurance. What odds I wonder would you have got if, in 1954, after his epic Wimbledon final against Jaroslav Drobny, you had backed him to reach the final again 20 years later?

Over the years as I have watched the giants of the past – men like Don Budge and Jack Kramer of America, the acrobatic Frenchman Jean Borotra, our own Fred Perry and those two extraordinary Australians Frank Sedgman and Lew Hoad, I have come to realize what enormous pressures they all faced – pressures which have become greater still since the advent of open tennis in 1968. Many, of course, succumb to the pressures and disappear from the game so that to me it is all the more remarkable that Ken Rosewall should not only have survived the years at the top of the world game, but should also have retained the same modest character, and the same humble approach to life as I well remember in the young man who came to practise at Wimbledon in 1952 at the age of 17. It speaks volumes for his upbringing, his utter professionalism, and his happy family life.

I can think of no finer example for young tennis players to follow in every aspect of the game than Ken Rosewall. Long may he continue to delight us.

INTRODUCTION

I was lucky I suppose that we had a tennis court at our home in Rockdale, a southern suburb of Sydney. In those days, during the last months of World War II, there were hundreds of private tennis courts dotted all over Sydney, as well as many clubs. Land was abundant and cheap so that it was not unusual for a family to have its own court beside the house – a situation that is disappearing fast today as land values rise. Flying over Sydney at night you used to be able to see dozens of floodlit courts – all with matches in progress. Tennis was the number one summer sport and the tennis clubs were social centres for the whole family. There were inter-club matches played in leagues, friendly matches and tournaments.

A proud 11-year-old with his first trophies outside our S. Huntsville home where the wall was the scene of many hours volleying practice.

I was 12½ when my mother took this picture at the White City Club in Sydney after I had won the NSW under-13 and under-15 singles titles.

Above: With Mervyn Rose, our manager Harry Hopman, and Lew Hoad at the All England Club, Wimbledon in May 1952 on my first overseas trip.
Left: At the Strathfield tournament, Sydney in 1950, one of the many metropolitan tournaments in which I learned the skills of match-play against some great Australians like John Bromwich and Adrian Quist.

My parents were both keen tennis players and I began to hit balls over the net quite early in life – I could not have been more than seven when I started. At that time, my father's racket was too heavy for me to hold easily, so I used to grasp it with two hands on the backhand side. I was probably a natural lefthander, but when my father decided I should try to play with one hand using a lighter racket, I settled for the right because I liked to swing the racket away from my body, holding the end of the handle with my right hand. Probably I would have had a more effective service today as a lefthander. Even now I can throw a ball more than twice as far with my left hand as with my right. This probably explains why my backhand side has always been stronger than the forehand. As I grew older and stronger I was able to manage the racket easily in my right hand alone and, like most tennis players, my racket arm became considerably more developed than my left arm.

When I was ten the family moved to South Hurstville and we were lucky to have a one-court club near by – the privately owned Wyanga Club – where the seniors must have been amused by my keenness to practise.

In all my tennis life my father has been my only teacher. As a player himself he was keen without being outstanding but he had read many books on the game and seen all the good Australians as well as outstanding overseas players like Fred Perry and Don Budge on their visits down under, He had the knack of transmitting what he had seen into sound guidance and preferred to see me control the ball well without trying to smite it too hard. With my somewhat light frame this was good advice and is something which I always remember when teaching youngsters myself. It is no good expecting a frail girl or boy to be able to control the ball when trying to hit it with the same power as a much stronger youngster. Physical development will always determine the type of game anyone is capable of playing. This is not to say that control has to come before power. Lew Hoad is a fine example of the husky boy who loved to hit the cover off the ball from an early age. With him power was natural and he had to learn to control his shots as he became more knowledgeable about the game. With me the physical power came only in my late teens though I managed to get pace on the ball by taking it early and timing it well.

Like all Australian children I had the opportunity to play tennis out of doors, all the year round, throughout my school days. Between the ages of nine and eleven I experienced my first taste of competitive play in local junior events for boys and girls organised by the Illawara Hard

Part of a victorious Australian Davis Cup team after our memorable victory against the Americans at Kooyong in 1953. l. to r. Rex Hartwig, Lew Hoad, Harry Hopman (captain), K. R., Mervyn Rose.

With Lew Hoad after my bitter-sweet victory against him in the US Championships final that was my revenge for defeats in Australia and Wimbledon but the end of his dream of the Grand Slam.

Court Tennis Association. By the time I was 13 I was playing regularly in school matches. We used to play at least twice each week and, of course, I would be out practising on the Wyanga court in the evenings and at weekends.

All of this doubtless helped me to understand something about match play, but I shall always think that my most valuable lessons were learned in the senior doubles matches I used to play with my father at weekends. Competing against adults in the local league competitions and knock-out cups was at the same time a challenge and a relaxation. I enjoyed pitting my growing skill against the superior strength and size of my adult opponents and there was never the same pressure on the results that began to creep into the junior events. Mind you, our senior opponents were not always exactly delighted if my father and I happened to beat them. Rivalry in these local affairs was intense and I can understand the frustration they must have felt at sometimes losing to a pint-size opponent and his father!

This period of my life was tremendous fun. Without realising it I was building up a wide circle of acquaintances and friends through my tennis, and many of those friendships have lasted to this day. As my game developed and I became lucky enough to travel overseas I began to realise what a truly international game tennis is. There is an infinite variety of tennis surfaces from the crushed shell courts of Manila to the dung courts of India and the immaculate turf of Wimbledon. There is variety too, in climatic conditions, from the tropic humidity of Kuwait to the blustery winds of Port Elizabeth in South Africa and the chill of a British spring at Bournemouth.

I have recently become more closely concerned with teaching the game to youngsters all over the world. In Britain and Australia I am, together with Rod Laver, Professional Adviser to the BP International Tennis Fellowship, and have conducted many playing clinics for them

Above: The start of my association with the BP International Tennis Fellowship in 1968 when Rod Laver and I met the two men who created the scheme – Julius Edwards of BP and John Barrett, the Director of the Fellowship.
Right: Demonstrating the service at one of the BP Fellowship's playing clinics at Aberdeen.

attended by the most promising juniors in Britain, Australia, and South Africa. Lately I have been teaching American children at the John Gardiner Tennis Ranch in the beautiful Camelback mountain area of Scottsdale, Arizona and I shall be conducting clinics for Cathay Pacific Airlines in the Far East.

One of the things I always tell these eager young players is that they are part of an enormous family. Tennis is probably the most widely played sport in the world and is enjoyed by both boys and girls, men and women from 8 to 80. Truly it is the game of a lifetime, to be enjoyed for its own sake as a pleasant and healthy social pastime or played as a competitive sport at all levels from club to championship. The possibilities are endless and, like all areas of human endeavour, the amount of pleasure one derives from it depends directly upon the effort put in. Also, unlike the team games learned at school – football, rugby, cricket, baseball, hockey, basketball, or netball – tennis can easily be enjoyed in later life. All you need is a court, a racket, some balls, and an opponent of about your own standard.

Another thing I have learned is that players who have taken the trouble to build their games on solid foundations at an early age have generally got more fun out of it than those who have tried to eradicate bad habits when they were older and less flexible. Habits in tennis are not easily broken so it makes sense to start out the right way. The right way will not necessarily be the same for everybody. We are all made differently – not only in the physical sense but also in outlook and temperament and in our ability to adapt to various ball games. Accordingly it is always sensible to discuss your background, attitude, ambitions and fears with a new coach before you begin any lessons, so that he may be able to give you proper advice about the way to approach your particular problems.

But before we get down to the details of how to hit the ball, let me tell you a little bit more about my own career – how the boy from Rockdale, who had always dreamed of one day playing in those prestigious tournaments in Australia, Europe, and America he had read about, suddenly found fantasy turning to reality as first he left Sydney for tennis matches in Melbourne at the age of 15 and then, three years later, travelled overseas with the Australian team to seek his fortune on the most famous courts in the world.

1. THE BIG FOUR

For most tennis players the thing they prize above all is victory in one of the four major world titles. By tradition the national championships of Australia, France, Great Britain, and the United States have achieved a status above all other events, and together make up the much-prized Grand Slam. While the development of tennis in the still relatively new open era might alter the emphasis by introducing newer and perhaps richer events, like the World Championship of Tennis for men and the Virginia Slims title for women, those four Championship meetings are likely to remain pre-eminent for some time yet. During the course of my career I've been fortunate enough to win three of the four, though the biggest one, Wimbledon, still eludes me. Each championship has its own special qualities and, for me, special memories which now stretch back over the past 25 years.

THE AUSTRALIAN CHAMPIONSHIPS

My first tennis trip to Melbourne was for the Victoria Championships in November 1949. It was the first time I had competed against men in a State Championship. I was just fifteen and my partner was none other than Lew Hoad, three weeks my junior. We were due to return to Melbourne two months later to represent New South Wales in the Linton Cup, the inter-state junior matches (under-19) played in conjunction with the national championships each year.

In January 1950 the Australian titles were to be played at the famous Kooyong Stadium in Melbourne and happily for us the New South Wales team won the Linton Cup that year. The Victoria Championships held at the same club in November had given Lew and I a wonderful opportunity to see some of the leading players of the world. We cheered on our own Frank Sedgman, Ken McGregor, Mervyn Rose, George Worthington, Geoff Brown, and Billy Sidwell and studied the stars from overseas like Jaraslov Drobny and Eric Sturgess. It amazed us, too, to see such expertise from the two visiting American ladies, Louise Brough and Doris Hart, who swept all before them in the ladies' events. Altogether it was an eventful few weeks in Melbourne for us both.

Above: With Lew Hoad on our first trip to Melbourne for the Victorian Championships of 1949. We were both nearly 15.
Right: Carrying the trophies of my first Australian Championship in 1956 was almost as much of a problem as beating Lew Hoad in the final.

In the national junior singles event that year I fought my way through to the final where I faced Peter Cawthorn, who had surprisingly beaten Lew in the semi-finals. By custom, the junior final was the last match to be played on the centre court, after the main finals. Because there had been some long matches, we started so late that bad light stopped us when I was trailing 1/3 in the final set – not a very happy situation.

As luck would have it, Melbourne's weather broke, and it rained practically without ceasing for a week. It seems amusing now to remember the frustration that Peter and I felt as we waited day by day for a chance to get our match finished. As it turned out we finished the match exactly one week later and fortunately for me I escaped from my difficulties and won that final set.

With the loss of so many leading Australian players to the professional ranks in the 1960s – in itself a compliment to the Australian tennis system – the Australian Championships lost some of their prestige. However, events since 1971 suggest that Australian officials are making up for the lost years and working constructively to build the home game towards its former greatness. During those lean ten years spectators have been scarce, but now they are thronging back as they have done for the past four years in Melbourne, where the Kooyong Stadium has been filled again for the first time since the 1950s. Sponsorship, too, is at last entering the Australian scene, and the circuit shows every sign of staging

a revival. Of course it does come at the end of a long circuit year for the leading players, many of whom will have contested the World Championship of Tennis circuit from January to May and then the Grand Prix Circuit. It is not possible for all of them to sustain the effort of high-level competition through the Christmas and New Year periods and it was no surprise in 1974 when 'Bill' Vilas and Ilie Nastase, the Masters' finalists in Melbourne, did not stay on for this Australian Open two weeks later.

The Australian Championships used to be played by rotation in the four main tennis centres, Sydney, Melbourne, Brisbane, and Adelaide. However, for the last three years they have been staged at Kooyong, which is developing into a first-class tennis centre. They have never been as big as France, Wimbledon, or Forest Hills and the draw has usually been restricted to 64 players. Like all summer tennis in Australia the Championships are played on grass courts. At most clubs the courts are of a high standard and the climate allows a long season. In Sydney, for example, the courts of the White City Club are used practically all the year round because there is enough space to rest courts that become worn. The sun burns all courts to a light brown colour in summer, but it also bakes the earth so that the surface is flat and the bounce is true.

Fortune has smiled upon me four times, in 1953, 1955, 1971, and 1972, but two players have brought the Australian Championships to public notice. In 1938 Donald Budge initiated the first Grand Slam in Australia, and Rod Laver has done so twice – as an amateur in 1962 and as a professional in 1969. To me this will always rank as one of the greatest feats of modern times when one considers the high level of entry he had to contend with at all four meetings. I wonder if we shall ever see it done again.

The great Rod Laver – the only man in history to have won the Grand Slam twice – in 1962 before tennis became Open, and in 1969, the second year of the new era.

THE FRENCH CHAMPIONSHIPS

My first visit to the leafy splendour of the Stade Roland Garros, set in a quiet corner of the Bois de Bologne near the Porte D'Auteuil, was in 1952 when Lew Hoad and I had our first overseas trip with an Australian team. We found the competition in Europe tougher than we expected because of the ultra-slow conditions and the patience and skill of the players who grew up on these slow clay courts. For us it was a new world and I was fortunate that my game suited this type of playing surface.

I've been lucky enough to play well in Paris and I have twice won the title there – on my second visit in 1953 and again in 1968 at the first French Open tournament. Like some of the other leading events in the world, the French Championship lost its prestige for a time due to the absence of the professionals and because of other competing events in a crowded international calendar. A hard-working and knowledgeable team of French officials led by former players Marcel Bernard, Philippe Chatrier, Pierre Darmon, and Benny Berthet, has for the past five years been working harder than ever to modernize the tournament.

Happily they have achieved some success despite being the victims of international tennis politics in 1972 when the WCT players were barred, again in 1973 when the 'Pilic affair' interrupted the smooth running of the tournament, and yet again in 1974 when they decided to ban all members of the new American 'World Team Tennis' league.

On my first visit in 1952 I was struck by the different styles all the Europeans employed – not like the serve and volley games of most Australians, but based on reliable ground strokes, patience, and a good pair of legs. Somebody once said that European players only come to the net once a match – for the final handshake. There is more truth in this jocular remark than you might think, and Australians by the score have come to realise the shortcomings of their own base-line games as they have tried to force the pace on these heartbreakingly slow courts. Looking back it was a remarkable achievement for Mervyn Rose to win the French title in 1958 because, despite a good serve, excellent volleys, and an outstanding overhead, Mervyn was never renowned for his ground strokes. Somehow, though, he hustled his way through the tournament as indeed Roy Emerson did in 1963 and 1967 by using similar methods.

Recently European players have become more aggressive so that experts like Jan Kodes of Czechoslovakia and young Bjorn Borg of Sweden thump the ball on both wings from the back of the court and come in repeatedly for volleying coups. Although Kodes is considered

Sweden's talented teenager Bjorn Borg, who became the youngest player ever to win one of the Big Four when he won the French Championships in 1974, a few days after his eighteenth birthday.

better on slow courts, he can play well on grass and did reach the final of the US Open in 1971 and won Wimbledon in 1973 largely on the strength of his service returns. Borg, who won the French title in 1974, has yet to prove himself on grass.

The spectators in Paris are always keen and often excitable – especially when there is a Frenchman to cheer. I have always found them reasonably fair and have enjoyed having them on my side more often than not. Perhaps in a Davis Cup match in Paris it would be different.

Like most other leading players, I find the clay court game much more satisfying. There is more scope for the full range of strokes which a fast surface does not allow. To most of us the fast court game is boring and we much prefer to pit our skills and our minds against one another on courts where the rallies can be developed. Forest Hills will be played on clay for the first time in 1975, and I really believe that even Wimbledon would be more rewarding for players and spectators on slower courts.

Most players would also agree that the French Championship title has always been the toughest one to win. Five set matches on slow clay against good runners in a field of 128 – often in high temperatures – take an awful lot of winning.

In my first French Championships in 1952 I lost to that remarkable Italian competitor, Fausto Gardini, in five sets. He said afterwards that he felt sure he would never beat me again – and he was right because we never met again! Lew and I got to the semi-finals of the doubles that year, beating Philippe Washer and Jackie Brichant, the Belgian Davis Cup pair, on the way. Many Europeans thought that was a good win for us, but we lost, perhaps inevitably, to Frank Sedgman and Ken McGregor who I rate as one of the best doubles teams of all time.

The Spanish left-hander Manolo Orantes, an expert on the slow clay of Europe, but yet to prove himself on the faster surfaces.

WIMBLEDON

Wimbledon! The very name conjures up a magical picture in the minds of all tennis players. To Lew Hoad and me, as we flew into London in April 1952 with the rest of the Australian team, Ken McGregor and Mervyn Rose, with Harry Hopman as our Captain/Manager, the prospects of practising there prior to our departure for France and the French Championships was exciting indeed.

Our arrival at the hallowed entrance in Church Road, and our entry through the Doherty gates lived up to every imagined picture. It was strange to see the towering creeper-covered Centre Court utterly deserted and no crowds thronging the walks which we knew so well from photographs, but it was a great treat for us to get a glimpse of the surroundings prior to the Championships. We were there for a few days of hard court practice but already the ground staff had groomed the grass courts to resemble thick, plush carpet. Mr Fuller, then head groundsman, told us that the warm spring rain had produced a good strong growth and he would soon be cutting down for the opening of the grass court season early in May. We had the friendliest of welcomes from Club Secretary Colonel Macaulay and all his staff and were tremendously impressed by the entire well-ordered scene.

I am sure that neither of us had dreamt when we started our tennis in Sydney that we might play there before our twentieth birthdays. Following the brief practice period, we left for Paris and after playing the Championships we returned to England for the pre-Wimbledon grass court tournaments at Beckenham and Queen's Club.

My first appearance at The Championships left me overawed. I played quite well but was a little nervous and lost to the American, Gardnar Mulloy in the second round – the tension and the atmosphere were somehow different, quite unlike anything I had experienced elsewhere. Wimbledon either inspires you or destroys you. I remember John Newcombe once saying that it took him six years to get past the second round.

It was such a thrill that first year seeing all the leading players in the world congregated before this appreciative and tightly packed audience. The management of the tournament was then, as it still is, superb, with every detail thought out to make it a pleasure for the spectators as well as the players. We had cars to take us to and from our hotel, wonderful changing facilities, and our own players' dining room where lunch and tea were provided. With the thronging crowds, press, TV and radio representatives from all over the world plus the unique garden party setting, the sense of atmosphere was quite unmistakable.

Lew Hoad's mighty game brought him two Wimbledon titles (1956 and 1957). Here he demonstrates his classic backhand volley.

Two years later I felt much more at home and played some of my best tennis to reach the singles final where the old Wimbledon hero, Jaroslav Drobny, a talented Czech left-hander, beat me in four close sets – a match about which I shall have more to say later.

Then, in 1956, I found myself in the final again, this time facing my doubles partner, Lew Hoad. Once more I had to be content with second place as Lew's powerful hitting carried him to a four set win that gave him the third leg of his Grand Slam attempt. There was some consolation, though, in the doubles final where Lew and I beat the difficult Italian pair – the giant Orlando Sirola who stood 6ft 7in. and seemed impossible to pass or lob at the net, and his highly gifted partner Nicola Pietrangeli – surely one of the sweetest hitters of a tennis ball to come out of Europe. That was my last appearance at Wimbledon before I turned professional with Jack Kramer's group early in 1957.

On my return to Wimbledon for the professional tournament of August 1967 after a gap of 11 years, nothing had changed – except perhaps for even greater public interest and the improvement in technical facilities like scoreboards, results boards, and spectator accommodation. The following year Open tennis gave even Wimbledon a boost, and it was largely as a result of the All England Club's pressure behind the scenes that it came at all. Tennis has much to thank Wimbledon for.

The game has become so much bigger now with the Eastern European bloc, the South American nations, and all the smaller emergent countries sending players to compete. In all this growth Wimbledon has retained its position as the leading tournament in the world. To win the singles there everything has to be going for you – the luck, a good draw, and most of all, good play. Each major championship requires different qualities to win it – or rather the same qualities in a slightly different mix. In Australia you need fast reflexes, quick movement, and the ability to sustain a serve and volley game in sometimes tropic heat. In France you need groundstroke ability, the mental and physical stamina for long rallies and long matches, and tactical skill and experience. The same qualities will be needed at Forest Hills now that they have changed to clay, but up to 1974 you needed a philosophical acceptance of erratic bounces, the ability to re-adjust to those bounces, plus the stamina and volleying skill necessary on grass courts. For Wimbledon you need all these qualities plus something extra – the ability to play for the world's greatest title and to withstand the enormous pressures that that implies. You know at Wimbledon that everyone who matters is there and everything happens fast. It still remains the greatest test of all.

On my first visit I was fortunate to get on to the hallowed turf of the Centre Court – that velvet carpet where the ball comes through true, fast, and low. I must admit to a touch of Wimbledon nerves as I lost my singles to Gardnar Mulloy, but I was to get my revenge. Lew and I were forming into a good doubles pair and we did particularly well on that first visit. I shall always remember the way we beat second seeds Mulloy and Dick Savitt. For two 17-year-olds it was a great thrill.

In play on Wimbledon's famous centre court during the second Open there in 1969. Nowhere else is there quite the same atmosphere or the same meticulous organisation.

The grass courts at Wimbledon are some of the best in the world, but the sixteen courts used for the Championships take a terrific pounding. Many people think that grass will eventually disappear from the game through the ever-rising cost of maintaining good courts. Unfortunately the good ones are rare, and there are many places where I would cheerfully play on a truer surface. The world's present grass court circuit is limited to Australia, New Zealand, Great Britain, Ireland, and India. The recent decision to replace grass with clay at Forest Hills will inevitably kill the Eastern grass court circuit in America.

I doubt, however, that the All England Club will ever change, and there is no reason why they should. The members enjoy playing on the grass courts and the Club has the income to maintain them at a level of perfection found nowhere else. But grass cannot stand the wear and tear of a multitude of players day after day, so that as the game spreads and the demand for court space increases (in the same way that the demand for space on golf courses has risen dramatically) the grass court clubs will be forced to find alternative surfaces.

Of my four Wimbledon finals in 1954, 1956, 1970, and 1974 I shall have more to say later, but no remarks about this famous tournament would be complete without reference to the dramatic events of 1973.

That year, along with all the other members of ATP, I had been unable to compete at Wimbledon following the boycott resulting from the ILTF's suspension of Yugoslavia's Nikki Pilic who, it was alleged, had refused to play for his country in the Davis Cup. I had made the journey to England especially for Wimbledon and you can imagine my private thoughts as the dramatic events of the pre-Wimbledon week unfolded with the unsuccessful ATP attempt to secure an injunction, the endless ATP board meetings, the hostility of the press, and the strong feeling that was aroused even among the members of the All England Club, some of whom I spoke to as I laboured on the practice court polishing my game for what I surely thought was my last serious chance to win the elusive tournament. As everyone knows, the President of the ILTF, Allan Heyman, would not lift the suspension on Pilic and the boycott was imposed. Jan Kodes of Czechoslovakia won his title from another East European – Alex Metreveli of Georgia.

Little did I think as I arrived once more in England the following year that I would be involved in a fourth Wimbledon final at the age of 39. I had spent the previous two months playing Team Tennis for the Pittsburgh Triangles, and indoor one-set matches on a carpet court are hardly the ideal preparation for a serious Wimbledon challenge. Yet despite a lack of grass court practice, one of the wettest Wimbledons on record which concertina'd the programme, and one of the toughest draws I have ever faced, it somehow happened again. How I recovered from being a set and a service break down against the powerful American left-handed Roscoe Tanner, I shall never know; nor shall I ever understand the reason for the see-saw nature of my win in a gusty quarter-final on the Centre Court against my old foe, John Newcombe, and I shall always believe that fate took a hand to help me beat Stan Smith in the semi-final when he led by two sets to love and held a match point in the tie-break of the third set.

Nor am I likely to forget the wonderful, furious aggression of young Jimmy Connors in the final. Great though the disappointment of losing was, sad though it was to have failed those numberless loyal supporters who had been marvellously encouraging in previous matches, yet I was still proud just to have played my part once again in acting out the drama that is Wimbledon.

FOREST HILLS

The US Championships has always been one of the hardest to win, thanks to the tremendous enthusiasm and ability of the native American players who compete there and also because the growth of tennis in America, having accelerated fast in the past five years, has provided a focal point for the hopes of all tennis lovers there. Television coverage of the Championships, together with network coverage of the WCT events since 1971, is mainly responsible for bringing tennis to an ever-wider audience. Perhaps before long tennis will become a major spectator sport in America to rival football, baseball, and basketball. With prize money around $150,000, the US Open is the second richest Championship in the world and second only in prestige to Wimbledon.

The balls used in America are generally faster than at Wimbledon, but the grass courts were never really good enough for such a major event, hence the change to clay in 1975.

For years it was the practice of Australian teams playing at Forest Hills to live in a house close by the Club. This was a sensible step in New York in September where the heat and humidity is always oppressive. It meant that there was always somewhere to go to relax so that in those early years I used to enjoy the conditions and played reasonably well there. That first visit in 1952 produced memorable performances from both Lew and me. In one day Lew beat Art Larsen, who had won the Championship two years earlier, and I beat the number one seed, Vic Seixas, who had lost in the final in the previous year to Frank Sedgman. I suppose Lew and I had helped to clear Sedgman's path. At all events he won his second consecutive title in a canter. My win against Vic started me off on a run of eleven victories against him that ended most abruptly and disappointedly for me in the Davis Cup Challenge Round in 1954.

I remember losing to Mulloy again in the quarter finals in 1952. This time it was a very close five-set match, much better than our encounter at Wimbledon. I believe Lew lost to Frank Sedgman in the same round.

Somehow my game has always worked well at Forest Hills, especially my service returns. Perhaps the extra pace of the faster American ball has helped my serve a little, too. In later years I came to the net more and relied on a serve and volley game because it became clear that it was better if you didn't allow the ball to bounce on the soft and uneven grass. Little did I think in those early years that one day I would be writing my own page of history at the US Championships. . . .

. . . The applause was deafening. Even when I was towelling off behind the umpire's chair and collecting my rackets and sweaters together I was

In 1974 Jimmy Connors ruled the world with outstanding tennis on all surfaces that won him the titles of Australia, Wimbledon and Forest Hills.

conscious of the excited buzz of discussion as the Forest Hills crowd moved in their seats relieved, like I was, to be able to relax at last.

Glancing over at John Newcombe I saw that he was ready to leave the court so I fell into step beside him. As we made our way across the vast expanse of green towards the Stadium exit the applause built up again. A tingle of excitement swept over me – as it always does when you have won – and I realized I was in the final of the 1970 US Championships – a second appearance after a gap of 14 years.

Fortunately for me, John had not moved or reacted today quite as fast as when we met in the Wimbledon final in July. My own game had worked well. Despite the erratic bounce from the uneven grass courts that are a continual source of irritation to players in America, I had been returning the serves as well as I have ever done. Two days before against the American No. 1, Stan Smith, I had been seeing the ball really well and by returning his big, heavy serve with interest never allowed him to build up the control of the rallies as he likes to do. Today it had been the same. John Newcombe's heavy serves – made even more difficult to return because he was using a metal racket – never dominated me, so that I was able to make him work hard for every point he won. Fortunately my concentration lasted well, too, and I was able to win in straight sets, 6-3 6-4 6-3 to avenge that defeat in the Wimbledon final.

As we got through the marquee and fought our way to the pavilion past the hordes of eager autograph hunters my mind went back 14 years to the last occasion I had appeared in the US final.

In a strange way history had repeated itself. For a second time I had been given the chance to avenge a Wimbledon defeat. My opponent in that 1956 final had been my old friend and rival Lew Hoad who was on the last leg of the Grand Slam – having won the singles titles of Australia, France and Wimbledon. I had good reason to know all about that record because I had been his victim both in Australia and at Wimbledon. Lew and I usually had good matches when we met because of a distinct contrast of styles – his exciting early-ball power play against my more consistent and accurate driving. In those days, especially, I used to play most of the time from the back of the court so that on slow surfaces I usually beat Lew but on fast courts he had the edge. In that 1956 Wimbledon final Lew's pace was overwhelming and he won 6-2 4-6 7-5 6-4. Somehow I had snatched that second set but, despite elusive break-points, I could never get my returns going consistently or keep him away from the net at the vital moments. His anticipation and volley power that day were tremendous and brought gasps of admiration from the knowledgeable centre court crowd. My one chance had come in that tense fourth set. I led 4-1 and felt I was getting back into the match with a fair chance of winning. However Lew came back strongly and reeled off the next five games to win his title.

It was my second defeat at the last hurdle at Wimbledon. Two years before, in 1954, at the age of 19, I had gone down to the popular Czech lefthander Jaroslav Drobny after a memorable and exciting four set tussle. It was said afterwards that the crowd had been against me but if so I cannot say it bothered me. I have always found Wimbledon spectators to be among the fairest in the world. Who can blame them if they took to their hearts the well-loved figure of Drobny, who, for years, had been gracing the courts with his own particular brand of artistry.

Hoad's 1956 Wimbledon victory had made the Grand Slam a possibility for the first time since 1938 – the year in which the red-haired Californian Donald Budge had carried all before him. That Forest Hills final had all the elements of drama – the perfect climax to an intriguing year. Happily for me, on the day my touch and control worked as never before. I found myself punching Lew's fastest serves back with pace and control so that his volleys were hit from lower down than usual. My lobs were going well too and kept him guessing so that he was never quite sure how close to move into the net. The uneven bounce favoured me a little also because Lew liked to hit his ground strokes really early with lots of top spin – which is not easy unless the bounce is perfect. My flatter swing took the racket more through the flight path of the ball instead of across it and gave me better control on the bad bounces. Also I coped with the gusty wind better than Lew, perhaps because I was so used to windy conditions at the White City courts in Sydney.

When I had won 4-6 6-2 6-3 6-3 – almost an exact reversal of the Wimbledon score – my elation was tinged with a sadness that Lew had missed his Grand Slam. No-one would have worn the highest mantle of tennis achievement more deservedly – or more modestly – for Lew has been one of the game's truly great champions. At his best he was almost unplayable – and I often wonder just what heights he might have reached if a series of injuries to his back and toe had not forced him to curtail his professional career in his mid-twenties – before he had reached his peak.

My third Wimbledon chance came 14 years later – the match already referred to against John Newcombe. I had come over from America in good time to prepare for the change to grass courts and went first to Eastbourne for the Rothmans Open.

The true bounce of the fresh grass courts at Eastbourne and the relaxed seaside atmosphere seemed to suit me. I played well there and won the tournament from my old Australian friend Bob Hewitt who now lives in South Africa. This put me in the right frame of mind for Wimbledon and when I saw the draw on the Wednesday evening at Eastbourne I knew that I had a chance to do well if I could maintain my form.

The early rounds suggested that I was playing quite well and I beat the improving young American Tom Gorman in the fourth round which brought me against Tony Roche in the quarters. Tony had played beautifully to beat me in the first open Wimbledon in 1968 and so I was particularly relieved to find some of my best form this time to get past him in four sets, 10-8 6-1 4-6 6-2.

In the semi-final I faced Roger Taylor who had played so well earlier to beat the top seed Rod Laver and the US Davis Cup player Clark Graebner. Again I managed to get my returns of serve going well and got an early break in the third set to win another four setter, 6-3 4-6 6-3 6-3.

Above: The bewitching artistry of Rumania's Ilia Nastase has already won him the Championships of Italy, France, and America. He has the ability, but perhaps not the temperament, to add Wimbledon to the list.
Left: My second US title in September 1970 gave me almost more pleasure than my first in 1956, not because the rewards were greater but because I had proved to myself that, at the age of 35, I could still win when it mattered.

The final was tinged with nostalgia. Memories of 1956 and the match against Lew Hoad flooded over me as I walked out on that famous court on finals day to face John Newcombe. I tried to approach the match like any other and told myself it was no different but, of course, nothing else is quite like the Wimbledon final.

On the day the conditions were slightly different from those we had experienced previously. Whereas the dry spell had burnt up the courts, which were playing a little slower than usual – something which all the competitors seemed to like – the Centre Court, when we walked out, was slightly damp. Our feet made slight impressions in the court, and the lines were even a trifle slippery. I had been starting fast in most of my matches but this time both John and I were having difficulty with our timing. We both mis-hit several balls in the opening games and I was a little fortunate to win the opening set after being a service break down.

Apart from a period in the fourth set when I got right on top John played about the same all through. He was serving well – particularly on the big points – so that although I held something like 15 points to break service I only made three of them. I found concentration difficult, partly because of the occasion and partly because of the slow tempo at which the match was played between points. By the time the fifth set began I was feeling physically tired and my game fell a fraction so that John got off to a quick start. As his confidence grew I could not raise enough of a spark to throw him off balance and he emerged a very worthy winner of a hard fought match, 5-7 6-3 6-3 3-6 6-1. . . .

. . . This 1970 US semi-final against John Newcombe, then, had turned back the pages of tennis history 14 years. But this time there was an important difference – my revenge victory had not won me the title – it had merely taken me into the final to meet a fellow Australian – the gifted left-hander Tony Roche.

After the disappointment at Wimbledon this was a match I wanted to win more than anything that had gone before in a long season. I had had too many experiences in 1970 of being runner-up and here, at last, in the final of the richest open tournament so far staged, was my chance to prove to myself that I could still win the big ones.

Tony is always a difficult opponent. His spinning left-handed shots give very awkward angles so that I was glad to have my fellow Australian Ray Ruffels, another left-hander, to practise against as I had done at Wimbledon on the day I had beaten Tony. In the first set Roche was all over me. I was conscious of being a little tense and although I was timing the ball well I was not winning too many points or games. I made a good start in the second and soon levelled matters at set all. The third set was crucial. I had an early service break to lead 4-2 but lost my own serve for four all. The games moved towards the drama of the sudden-death tie-break. Fortunately I managed two good shots in the play-off and an unusual error from Tony on the volley gave me the 5-2 margin and the vital two sets to one lead.

When I won Tony's opening serve in the fourth set I knew that it would be my day if I could only maintain my form. I concentrated on getting in close behind my serve and not doing too much with the volley unless I was sure I could hit a winner. The games moved to 5-3 and the first match point arrived. I followed in fast and there was the ball coming at me on the forehand side waiting for me to move across for the forehand volley. Two quick steps and I punched it out of Tony's reach just inside the far side line. I had done it after a gap of 14 years! I had won the US title – the last of the major events of the year.

2. BEFORE WE BEGIN

I am going to assume that the reader has a working knowledge of the rules of lawn tennis, which includes the dimensions of the court, the height of the net, and the method of scoring.

Before I discuss the strokes of the game individually in detail I will consider some of the other factors which apply to all players, like the choice of a suitable racket and sensible clothing, movement, footwork, balance, the stroke itself, and recovery.

EQUIPMENT AND CLOTHING

Choose a racket with care to suit your physique. It should be heavy enough to give you all the power you can impart without being in danger of breaking, and light enough to wield quickly and easily. With the increasing pace of the modern game there is a tendency for leading players to like lighter-headed rackets than they used to. The best person to advise on the choice of racket is your coach or local retailer, who will explain that rackets are made in a wide range of weights ($12\frac{1}{2}$ oz–15 oz approximately), grip sizes (4 in.–5 in. approximately) and balances, and at all prices.

Nowadays there is a choice between wooden, metal (steel or aluminium alloy), fibreglass, carbon fibre, or composite frames. My advice to beginners is to start with a wooden racket made by a reputable company, strung with one of the best synthetic strings for longer wear. At this stage the faster pace generated by other rackets and natural gut, with consequent loss of control, can be a disadvantage. Later on when your shots are grooved, change to natural gut stringing which will give you greater response and 'feel' than synthetic strings. For really talented players it is possible to get amazing 'feel' even with synthetics. I always convince any who doubt the truth of this remark by reminding them that the great American player Art Larsen, who won the US Championships in 1950, and was one of the finest controllers of a tennis ball I have ever seen, always played with rackets strung with nylon-based synthetic strings. In the days when he was an opponent of mine I was only relieved that no-one bothered to explain to him the advantages of natural gut!

A change to metal, fibreglass or one of the carbon frame rackets should not be attempted too early. The quicker flexing properties of these other materials means that the ball stays less time on the strings than it does with a wooden frame, so that experience and control of every shot is necessary to use them with effect. All too often one sees inexperienced players wielding expensive rackets, quite unable to control the ball. Human nature encourages them to remember the few spectacular winners and forget the frequent extravagant errors. To sum up, it is generally true that metal, fibreglass or carbon rackets exaggerate everything. The good shots become better and the bad shots worse. Accordingly you must be at the stage where you are confident of hitting more good shots than bad to make the change.

The grip size of a racket is entirely a personal matter. There are no hard and fast rules save only that comfort comes before everything. You should feel that your hand can grip the handle firmly with the fingers comfortably spread and the whole racket under control. Although my own hand is small I feel comfortable with a grip that measures almost five inches, which is large by any standard. By contrast the famous Australian double-hander, John Bromwich, from whom I learned a great deal about the game in my formative years, used a very light racket with a tiny grip that measured less than four inches.

The rackets I use today have hardly altered from the model I used when I was 16. Ever since that time they have been made for me to the same specifications by the Slazenger Company in Sydney. The dimensions are – weight: $14\frac{1}{2}$ oz, balance (measured from the end of the handle): $13\frac{3}{16}$ in., grip size: $4\frac{15}{16}$ in., gut tension: 48 lb–52 lb (depending upon playing conditions).

Many promising young players mistakenly believe that the leading players have their rackets strung board tight – something over 65 lb – to get power and pace of shot. A few big servers like Mike Sangster have preferred tight stringing but the majority prefer a medium tension or, like myself, a lower tension so that the ball stays longer on the strings for greater control. John Newcombe, for instance, has his rackets strung at 48 lb at Wimbledon and I can assure you from personal experience that his shots are not lacking in power.

When selecting tennis balls it is a false economy for all except absolute beginners to select cheap grade ones. The covers wear smooth much sooner so that control becomes difficult. Any leading brand of top grade balls will give you far greater enjoyment for longer and will be controllable too.

Nowadays there is an ample choice of well designed clothing available for men and women that is both functional and attractive. I always try to

John Newcombe's lunging forehand volley emphasises that tennis is an athletic game full of violent movement.

see that my own clothing is clean and pressed when I play as a mark of respect for my opponent. There is no place for sloppily dressed players in the modern pro. game and, with modern fabrics there is no reason why players at all levels should not wear bright, clean clothes.

I try to apply the same standards of cleanliness to my shoes which are light, with canvas uppers, and have a patterned sole that provides a good grip on all surfaces. Again, comfort is the key factor. Try to find a shoe that fits snugly so that the foot does not move about inside – a common cause of blisters.

MOVEMENT

Tennis is essentially a game of movement. As in all direct combat sports like squash, badminton, table tennis and even boxing and fencing, your opponent is trying to make things as difficult as possible for you. Similarly you are trying to outwit him by placing the ball where he least enjoys playing it, making him run, stretch, twist, and turn so that he is never quite sure what you will do next. You only have to watch a match between two good players to realise how much ground they cover and how quickly they react to every move by their opponent.

We are all born with different natural abilities for movement but, for all of us, there are ways to improve upon nature. The most practical way to produce faster movement on a tennis court is to find an opponent who is better than you are – someone who hits the ball faster and closer to the lines than your usual opponent. Not only will you have to move faster but also your own shots will be put under greater pressure than usual, a basic form of training used by all the best players to quicken their reactions which I shall be discussing later on.

Speed about the court is closely allied to strength and anticipation. I shall be talking about strength later, but anticipation is something which everyone can acquire from the beginning with a little thought and application.

Anticipation is a combination of knowledge and confidence. Knowledge comes from watching the sort of shot your opponent likes to hit in certain situations. Perhaps he will invariably hit his backhand passing shots down the line or maybe he always lobs when running for wide forehands. In either case a little study of his game will give you the confidence to move into position for your volley or smash before the ball is hit. On a few occasions, of course, he will leave you standing by changing his pattern and hitting a different shot, but the percentage of winners to losers will make the exercise well worthwhile.

If you have not seen your opponent play before, build up in your mind a pattern of his behaviour on various shots as the match progresses. In this way you can begin to anticipate his replies in given situations and move confidently and early into position to hit the next shot. During the rallies themselves as soon as you have hit the ball watch your opponent, not the ball, and see how he shapes to hit his shots. With experience you will begin to know where he is going to hit the ball from the way he prepares and, once again, you will be able to move with confidence to the right place.

Although Arthur Ashe is leaping to hit this mid-air volley, his whole body remains in perfect balance.

FOOTWORK

Footwork is a vital part of every shot. Anticipation and movement will carry you towards the right part of the court to meet the oncoming ball but unless the footwork is sound the shot you play will not be effective.

Unlike a golf ball which is stationary and in approximately the same place relative to your body for every shot, the tennis ball arrives at a different speed and height every time, depending upon the shot your opponent has hit and the court surface you are playing on. Sometimes the ball will skid through low, sometimes it will dig in and bounce up slowly and occasionally it will die away quietly, hardly bouncing at all.

Accordingly it becomes imperative to adjust to the position of the ball so that every shot can be hit at a comfortable height. The ideal height for ground strokes (forehand and backhand drives) is level with the hip and the purpose of footwork is to allow you to hit ground strokes at hip level regardless of the type of ball you have to play. Volleys are easiest to hit between waist and chest height and smashes are managed most easily about three to four feet above your head.

One of the things that beginners often find difficult is to judge where the ball is going to bounce and what it will do after bouncing. One is always seeing beginners swotting at the ball level with their heads or scooping with their rackets at balls well in front of them. I know when I take my own two boys, Brett and Glenn, out on the court, I am constantly having to remind them to move back five or six paces for high, bouncing balls or forward for the short ones.

If you do find this a problem go out on court with a friend and take it in turns to put your racket aside and try to move to the shots he hits over the net so that you catch the ball after it has bounced and at hip height. It is sometimes easier to concentrate on one thing at a time like this without bothering about what to do with the racket and once the habit has been formed you should be able to move properly to the right place with the racket in your hand.

Though the details of footwork for each shot vary a little the underlying principle is the same for all shots. You should aim to play every shot at a convenient height and with your weight moving forward so that your racket meets the ball out in front of you and carries you into the shot.

When I am waiting to return service I like to lean slightly forward from the waist with knees slightly bent and with my weight on my toes so that I can move off fast in any direction. If I have hit the ball in a rally and am waiting to see where it will come back I still keep my weight forward on my toes and move with light skipping movements.

The next time you watch good players do not follow the flight of the ball but keep your attention directed on the feet of one of them. You will see how flexible and fluid his whole movement is and how he tries to get himself into a comfortable position to make each shot by moving backwards or forwards and from side to side with short, powerful steps.

BALANCE

As I have already mentioned there is an endless variety of shots that a tennis player has to make during the course of a match and good balance is an essential part of his repertoire. Just as the skier is constantly adjusting his balance to meet the ever changing demands of the slope so a tennis player is constantly altering his balance as he chases and lunges, leaps and twists all over the court. Because he carries a racket and usually hits the ball out to one side the tennis player needs to maintain his balance by using his free arm in the same way that a skier uses his sticks. In addition he must be supple and flexible so that the whole body adjusts to the changing demands of balance as each shot is played. The position already mentioned – with the weight forward on the toes and the knees slightly bent and the racket supported lightly at the throat with the free hand – is the starting point for every ground stroke and volley.

These are things which come naturally to most people but may need some attention from those players who tend to be stiff in movement and cramped in style, with the free arm glued to the side of the body. I often find that relaxation is the missing factor with such players. They are trying too hard. Once they have consciously relaxed their muscles the awkwardness disappears and balance follows naturally.

THE STROKE ITSELF

Every shot in the game has three distinct phases which, when performed by an expert, blend into one continuous and often beautiful movement – they are preparation, execution and finish.

As the player is moving about the court and adjusting his footwork to the demand of the ball his opponent has just hit he should be starting the **preparation** of his own shot. Assuming the ball is coming down the centre of the court this means he will be getting the racket back early in the same plane of flight as the oncoming ball, turning away from the waist until he is sideways to the net and watching the ball closely.

If the preparation has been achieved properly the **execution** will follow naturally. As the weight moves forward on to the front foot the straight arm and racket swing forward with braced wrist to meet the ball at the side and slightly in front of, the body.

The **finish** of each shot is the factor that ensures full control of the

ball and gives a satisfying solidity to the shot. On ground-strokes I always try to swing my racket forward through the path of the ball and finally up to shoulder height at least. On volleys it is the abbreviated punch with no follow through that gives crispness and pace to the shot – so again the finish gives the shot its quality. On services and smashes the full follow through again adds the control factor as well as ensuring that the shot carries maximum power.

RECOVERY

One of the things which distinguishes a good player from a mediocre one is the way he moves after making his shot. How often have you seen a poor player lose the point to a simple return that he could easily have reached because he stood admiring his latest brilliant forehand assuming that it was a winner?

But watch the good player and see how he sets off immediately he has hit his shot, either towards the place where he expects his opponent to hit the ball (and he is occasionally wrong!) or to the 'neutral' position one yard behind the centre of the baseline.

FROM THE CONSCIOUS TO THE SUBCONSCIOUS

In the pages that follow I will try to explain how I believe the strokes of the game should be hit to get the maximum effect with the minimum of effort and error. There is always room for personal interpretation of the fundamental principles involved in the production of each shot – one only has to look at the different styles which the leading players have developed – so that one should not attempt to follow the instructions too slavishly. Treat the points I make as guide lines and put your own interpretation on them.

One of the problems which faces anyone attempting to learn a new skill is the difficulty of trying to co-ordinate a series of complicated movements on the conscious level. From my own experience with golf I know how hard it can be to co-ordinate the individual points so that they become a harmonious whole. All one can do is to offer the encouraging truth that with constant repetition and practice the whole process eventually removes itself from the conscious level to the subconscious, at which time it is possible to think about the other tactical elements of the game.

In tennis we usually refer to this learning process as 'grooving the swing'. It is sometimes a help to carry out this practice in front of a mirror

In America with my sons Glenn and Brett, whose own tennis problems have helped me to learn new techniques of teaching.

so that you can see if the visual picture of what you are doing fits your mental picture. Even more effective is to use a video tape recording machine – which we always do at the BP clinics – so that you can hit a whole series of shots and see the results immediately afterwards.

Finally, I believe that the best coaches and teachers are the ones who guide and mould the natural stroke production of a player without making wholesale changes for the sake of perfection. There are many roads to heaven – all of them littered with the corpses of those who have sacrificed natural flair for technical excellence.

However, from the pages of a book I am unable to see just what natural talent you, as an individual, have. Accordingly I have tried to keep my advice simple and straightforward because I believe that the game is easier to learn if you have only the skeleton before you and clothe it with your own flesh and blood.

HOW TO HOLD THE RACKET

One of the most difficult aspects of tennis about which to offer advice without having personal knowledge of the player's game concerns the grips to use for the various strokes. Although there are grips that are generally accepted as 'normal' the leading players employ such a large number of variations that it becomes difficult to decide what to say to beginners. On reflection, however, this knowledge should provide encouragement to beginners because, obviously, the champions must have started their careers as beginners themselves, when they were probably taught the 'correct' grips, and have since adapted the basic rules to suit their own individual styles and requirements.

If you are a complete beginner, then, I would advise you to try out the grips I suggest for beginners. They are most likely to give you power and control on your shots.

If, however, you have progressed from the first stage and developed a particular shot of your own, say a forehand drive, in which you have confidence then, even if the grip is unorthodox, go on using it.

Perhaps you are having trouble on another shot – say the backhand drive – which is possibly erratic and lacking in control. The chances are that you are using the same grip as for the natural forehand and a change to something more orthodox would improve the stroke.

The real point I am trying to convey is that, within certain limits, there is room for personal adjustment in the way to hold the racket – the experiences of champions proves that.

Only Lew Hoad's immense physical strength enables him to play all his shots with one grip – beginners please note.

MY OWN GRIPS

For all my shots I use only two grips: one for the forehand drive; the other for every other shot I play – backhand drive, all volleys, service and smash. I will describe them both in a moment. Thus, for me, there are few complications and there is little to go wrong. Some players, like Lew Hoad, use only one grip for all their shots, and when you remember that nowadays the ball is being hit harder and faster than ever (particularly by the metal racket users) in the quest for ever-growing prize money, the one-gripper has a slight advantage over players who make a change.

Before you all decide to rush out on court using only one grip for all your shots – a word of warning. Lew Hoad is able to hold his racket this way only because he is immensely strong, especially in the wrist. It would be madness for any girl or a young boy to set out as a one-grip player. They would not have the physical strength to control the racket properly. This is what the problem is all about, holding the handle of the racket so firmly that when the strings meet the ball the head of the racket is not deflected from its path but moves on solidly through the flight path of the ball.

MY FOREHAND GRIP

For my forehand drive I use the 'shake hands' grip sometimes called the 'Eastern'. My version is the Australian one with the 'V' between thumb and forefinger on top of the handle and the large knuckle of the first finger on the right-hand corner of the handle as you look down on it yourself – as you can see from the drawings. The palm is slightly behind the handle and the fingers are spread to give support and solidity when meeting the ball.

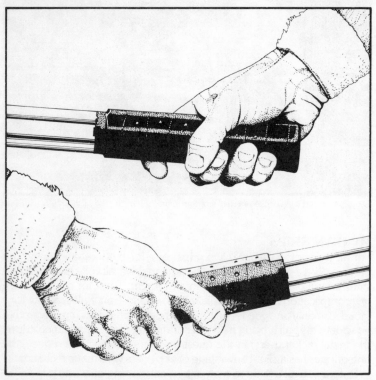

Two views of my own forehand grip, the 'Eastern'. You can see that the forefinger is spread and the thumb wrapped round the handle for firmness.

Allowable Alternative

The American version of this 'Eastern' grip, as used by Jack Kramer and Stan Smith, for example, has the palm rather more behind the handle. This method provides even greater solidity but involves a larger change for backhand shots.

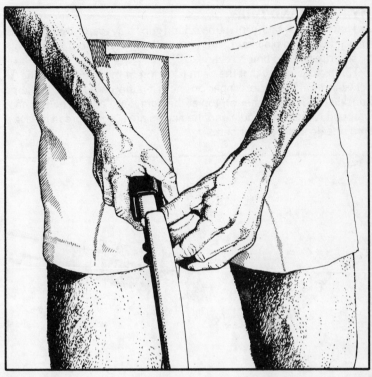

My forehand grip viewed from in front. Notice that I am shaking hands with the handle.

Beginners

Use either version of the 'shake hands' grip, whichever feels more comfortable. To find this grip easily hold the racket in front of you with your free hand with the head in the vertical plane edgeways to the ground and the handle pointing at your tummy. Now place your playing hand flat on the strings and slide it down the shaft towards the grip until the heel of your hand is just touching the raised butt at the end of the handle. Wrap your fingers and thumb around the grip keeping the fingers spread. You are now literally 'shaking hands' with the handle.

In my remarks about equipment on page 37 I mentioned the importance of choosing a racket with a handle size that feels comfortable. Obviously if the fingers dig into the fleshy part of the hand below the thumb then the grip is probably uncomfortable and too small. Equally if the fingers can hardly wrap round the handle the grip will be uncomfortable and insecure because it is too big.

MY BACKHAND GRIP

As I have already said, with my backhand grip I play every other shot and, in fact, I can also play forehand drives with it, which I do if I am caught by surprise with no time to change.

The pictures show that the palm is on top of the handle with the 'V' between thumb and forefinger on the left-hand corner and the large knuckle of the first finger on top at the right-hand edge. The thumb is wrapped round the handle and the fingers are slightly spread to give a comfortable feeling of support.

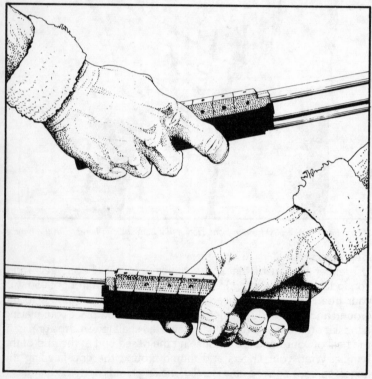

My backhand grip viewed from the front and back. This is the same 'Continental' grip that I use for serving and volleying so that I have versatility in mid-rally.

This is sometimes called the full 'continental' grip for which I move my hand about a quarter of a turn to the left from my forehand grip, a small change which is not difficult to make in play.

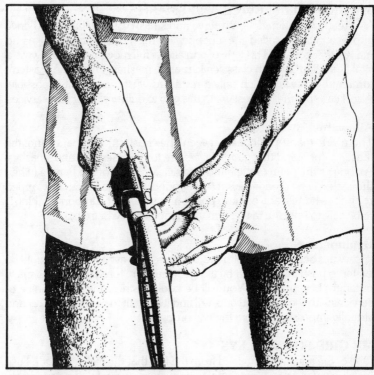

A head-on view of my backhand grip which enables me to hold the racket firmly.

Allowable Alternative

A widely taught grip is the 'Eastern' backhand for which the hand is a shade further to the left than in my grip, with the large knuckle of the first finger on top of the handle towards the centre and the thumb spread at an angle across the back of the handle for support.

Beginners

Use whichever of the above versions feels more comfortable. Girls and young boys who have not yet acquired full strength will probably find the 'Eastern' backhand easier because of the extra support given by the thumb. If the racket still feels unwieldy then try holding the racket further up nearer the head. This 'choking-up' on the grip is a useful temporary expedient to give a greater feeling of control.

MY GRIP FOR SERVICE AND SMASH

As already mentioned, I both serve and smash with my backhand drive grip – sometimes called the 'chopper' or full 'continental' grip – as do many other players. This type of grip allows full movement of the wrist, a vital ingredient of high class services and smashes, unlike the 'Eastern' forehand grip with which only a restricted wrist movement is possible. Also, I can spin the ball easily with this grip to deliver slice or kick services.

Allowable Alternatives

There are many positions between the 'Eastern' backhand and the 'Eastern' forehand that good players use for their services and smashes. As long as the palm of the hand is basically on top of the handle (when the racket is held edgeways to the ground) and the thumb is wrapped round the handle any of these positions is sound. The important thing is to be able to hold the racket firmly and move the wrist freely.

Beginners

It is always better to start with the 'chopper' grip even though it might be easier to push the ball over by using an 'Eastern' forehand grip, as many untaught beginners do. You will be badly restricted in your choice of services with the forehand grip, will find it difficult to generate power and virtually impossible to spin the ball properly.

MY GRIP FOR VOLLEYS

One of the advantages gained from the fact that the backhand grip I use for all my volleys is a 'continental' grip, short of the full 'Eastern' backhand, is that all my forehand volleys can be hit just as comfortably.

This is not the case for players who use a full 'Eastern' backhand grip; for them it is impossible to hit forehand volleys effectively. Accordingly most of these players use their service grip, the 'chopper' or 'continental' like I do for both forehand volleys and backhand volleys. This involves them in the use of three grips in all – 'Eastern' forehand for forehand drives, 'Eastern' backhand for backhand drives and 'chopper' for serving, smashing and volleying.

Beginners

Try to start with the 'chopper' grip from the beginning. You will be learning to serve with this grip, too, so it will be familiar to you. If you find it difficult to control the racket in the short, sharp, punching action I shall be describing later as ideal for volleys then try holding it a little higher up the handle. As with the backhand drive this temporary 'choking-up' on the grip helps to bring confidence through greater firmness on impact.

3. THE GROUNDSTROKES

THE STROKES OF THE GAME

In this section I will describe how I hit my shots and try to help you with yours by explaining the simple theory that lies behind each and the errors that commonly creep in. I have confined my remarks to the basic shots of the game, believing that once they are mastered the additions and variations involving the use of spin and 'touch' readily follow. Although, for the sake of convenience, I refer to right-handed players only all the remarks apply equally to left-handers who should merely transpose right for left and left for right as they read.

THE GROUND STROKES

The whole object of starting to play tennis is to derive enjoyment and recreation from the game and this will be achieved only when you can maintain a rally with an opponent. Accordingly, an understanding of the basic requirements for hitting forehand and backhand drives will pay the quickest dividends in terms of enjoyment and satisfaction.

Ground strokes are swinging strokes where the head of the racket is swung through the ball. I will explain how to prepare for the drives so that you can swing the racket freely throughout the entire stroke.

Fundamentally forehands and backhands should be hit with a low backswing and a high follow through. In preparation the racket should be pointing at the fence behind you and after you have swung it through to hit the ball it should finish pointing high at the fence in front of you. Let me now tell you in more detail how footwork, racket swing and body movement are all co-ordinated to produce smooth, powerful shots.

BACKHAND DRIVE

I begin with the backhand drive for a special reason that I hope will kill a myth. Many beginners believe, for some reason, that backhands are particularly difficult to master, and some are even frightened to attempt them. Most club players will automatically direct their shots to an unknown opponent's backhand because of a subconscious belief that it will be weaker than his forehand. If this is true at lower levels of the game it is probably because beginners spend more time hitting forehands than backhands, with a consequent strengthening of the 'grooving' on the forehand side, and not because there is intrinsically anything more

The complete backhand stroke which combines all the qualities of footwork, balance, and early preparation to get the player into the right place.

difficult about hitting backhands.

The myth of backhand difficulty is exploded completely at the highest levels of the game where we find more players with stronger backhands than forehands. Rod Laver, perhaps, has an equally good forehand but Tony Roche, Roy Emerson, Fred Stolle, Arthur Ashe, Andres Gimeno, Jimmy Connors, Chris Evert, Margaret Court, Billie-Jean King, Nancy Richey, Maria Bueno, Evonne Goolagong and many others all have stronger backhands – as I do myself.

Reference to my remarks about movement, footwork, and balance will remind you that positioning is all important for hitting consistent backhands.

Preparation

As soon as you realise that the ball is coming at you on the backhand side keep your eyes glued to it until after you have hit the shot. Decide where you will have to move to so that, after the ball has bounced, you will be able to hit it at hip height. With practice, small, quick steps (adjusting with skip steps as necessary) will take you to the right place in time and this phase of the shot will eventually become automatic.

As you start to move to the right place begin the preparation of the shot by first changing to your backhand grip, then turning sideways at the waist away from the net while supporting the throat of the racket lightly with the left hand and watching the ball over your right shoulder.

The racket should be taken back in the same plane of flight in which you expect to hit the ball while you are estimating its pace and trajectory through the air on its way to you. If you are playing on a fast surface like grass or wood and expect the ball to skid through low, then bend your knees and take the racket back in a low plane as you start to turn sideways and move towards your hitting spot.

If you expect the ball to bounce high and have enough time move back quickly, taking the racket back at hip height, so that your hitting spot will allow you to meet the ball at the comfortable hip height. If you have no time to move back then take the racket back in the high plane to meet the expected flight of the ball after it has bounced.

Always take the racket back early with a firm wrist.

Execution

If your positional sense has been accurate you will be in a perfect position to move into the shot meeting the ball as you move forward and across on to the right foot, and striking the ball slightly in front of you. *As the racket swings forward keep the arm straight and the wrist braced so that it is in a straight line and, as you swing, turn at the waist back towards the net so that the swing is unrestricted and free.*

Finish

The moments after the solid impact with the ball are vital to control. A high speed film of a tennis shot reveals that the ball stays on the strings for several thousandths of a second during which time the ball flattens and the strings stretch behind the frame which, itself, bends considerably.

Thus the finish of the shot needs to be as solid as the execution: the whole racket being carried through the intended flight path of the ball with arm still straight and wrist still braced. If the racket is carried like this to shoulder level or even head height the vital control factor will be built into the shot.

Although I have broken the stroke up into three phases it becomes one harmonious movement when played properly and contains all the balance, rhythm and timing that are features of a well hit shot.

It always gives me satisfaction when I time the ball really well and hit it cleanly. There have been many key backhands in my career that I was fortunate enough to time properly but none more dramatic than one I hit on my first visit to Wimbledon in 1952 at the age of 17. My tennis twin, Lew Hoad, and I were on the famous centre court for the first time in our young lives, excited and a little nervous to find ourselves playing the second seeded pair in the men's doubles, the Americans, Gardnar Mulloy and Dick Savitt. This was a third round match and the winners would be in the quarter finals – a thrilling prospect for us. The match had started well. We had won the first two sets but lost the third and fourth finding the guile and experience of Mulloy an effective foil for the powerful hitting of Savitt, who was the reigning Wimbledon champion.

With the games level in the final set and the rallies tense, Mulloy hoisted a lob over us as we were both moving forward. I realised, almost too late, that Lew was not going for it and set off for the baseline and the open area beyond. I met the ball about ten feet behind the line and swung desperately at it almost before it had bounced, with my back still to the net. Fortunately I must have just timed it perfectly for the early-hit backhand projected the ball like an arrow between the surprised Americans who did not even begin to move to cover the shot. We did not look back from that moment and much to our surprise and delight went on to win the match 6-4 8-6 1-6 3-6 7-5.

Stan Smith leans on this backhand return of serve beautifully. He will meet the ball well out in front of him moving forward and his firm wrist and intense concentration will make it a solid shot.

FOREHAND DRIVE

The forehand drive is almost a mirror image of the backhand except that the racket is further from the body so that you can reach wider balls more easily.

Preparation

Preparation for this stroke follows the same principles as for the backhand. Again, the key feature is the footwork which must carry you accurately and quickly to the place where you expect the ball to be at hip height after it has bounced.

When the ball leaves your opponent's racket take your eyes off your opponent (whose whole manner will have told you to expect a shot on the forehand side) and fix them on the ball until after you have made your shot.

On your way to meet the ball you should first change to your forehand grip and then start turning from the waist to the right, away from the net, taking the racket back in the plane of flight in which you expect to hit the ball. *Always take the racket back early with a firm wrist until it is pointing at the fence behind you.*

Execution

As the ball approaches the position where you want to meet it step forward and across with the left foot while swinging the racket firmly through the flight path you want the ball to follow. This forward motion will carry your body weight into the shot and *contact will be made slightly in front of you, with the racket and arm in a straight line and the wrist firmly braced.* The swing will unwind your shoulders so that on impact you are facing the net.

Finish

Once again it is imperative to stay with the shot and *carry the racket smoothly on through the path of the ball, still with a firm wrist, until the straight arm swings the racket up to shoulder or head height until it is pointing at the front fence.* This firm follow-through will give the shot its vital control.

THE BACKSWING

I generally use a shorter backswing on my own forehand drive now than I used to. When my father taught me he had been watching the full backswings of Perry and Budge and gave me the same full swing. However, when I joined the professional ranks in 1957 I found that I had no time to play the shot properly. I was constantly being hurried, especially

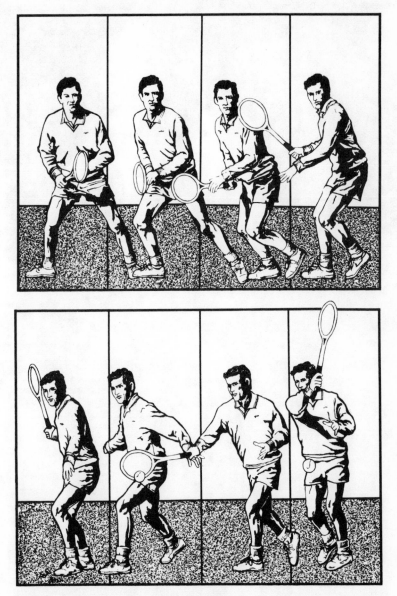

The forehand drive, like the backhand, depends upon the coordination of footwork, balance, and early preparation so that the racket head can be swung smoothly at the ball.

by Pancho Gonzales' heavy service. Accordingly I found it necessary to abbreviate the backswing on fast courts and this has had the effect of making the whole stroke feel much more compact and secure and less risky.

With the increased pace that metal rackets are bringing to the game I believe that this tendency for shorter backswings will spread at the top level of the game where many tournaments are played on fast synthetic carpet courts, grass, cement, or wood.

In Europe the slow clay courts give ample time for full backswings and, indeed, they are necessary if a player is going to hit powerful shots without forcing from an inadequate preparation. This is one reason why young players bred on European clay find it so difficult to time the ball on fast courts. Until they shorten their swings their problems will remain.

I find I have to be adaptable, altering the length of my backswing to suit the court speed. However, the beginner need worry only about getting the racket back early and can let the extent of the backswing take care of itself. Initially, it is better to have the racket back too far, waiting for the ball to arrive, rather than have to rush the whole stroke by being too late. The correct timing of the whole swing, and the degree of backswing necessary for the court being played on, (which will depend upon the opponent's pace of shot) will come with practice and experience.

I was never more relieved that my preparation for a forehand had been done early than in the 1970 US Open final at Forest Hills. Against Tony Roche, with the score at set all, I lost an early service break lead in the third set and the games reached 6-all which meant a sudden-death nine point tie-break. This system may be thrilling for the spectators, but for the players it can be nerve-wracking in the extreme. Tony, I remember, missed a relatively easy backhand volley – most unusual for him – to give me a lead of three points to two. On the next point Tony came in and punched a fast volley to my forehand side. I sped across with my racket already back and hit a running forehand sharply across the court past him for a winner. That shot gave me a 4-2 lead and virtually the third set. They do not often happen like that.

Practice for Ground Strokes
Until the swings are 'grooved' practise them regularly in front of a mirror or, if possible, in conjunction with video-tape equipment. There is nothing so instructive as seeing for yourself what the stroke looks like.

At the point of impact on this forehand I am still moving forward on to my left foot. Try not to let a deep ball drive you back so that you hit the ball leaning backwards. You will lose power and sky the ball if you do.

Frank Sedgman has prepared early for this forehand drive so that he can step into the shot as he swings the racket forward to meet the ball. Notice that he watches the ball intently and uses his left arm for balance.

At the learning stage keep on checking that your grip has not altered unintentionally. The object must be to 'groove' the whole process of producing the stroke until it is no longer a conscious act. This takes many hours of patient application and informed guidance.

Once the stroke is 'grooved' build up consistency and control by placing targets in the corners of the court (a one yard square is suitable) and try to hit them during rallies with a like-minded opponent.

Practise the cross-court drives and then down-the-line drives one at a time and turn it into a competition by keeping the score of targets hit.

As confidence develops get your opponent to stand at the net on one side of the court and direct your drives at him. After a while get him to stand the other side and continue the practice. You will now have half the time to prepare your strokes and will be improving movement, footwork and balance while you practise both forehand and backhand. If the stroke tends to break down when your opponent is volleying it means that your 'grooving' is not quite ready for making the whole stroke more quickly so revert to the original practice, with your opponent on the baseline, for a little longer. The more advanced 'threes' practice I shall be describing later.

COMMON ERRORS

Wristiness
If the wrist is not braced at impact the stroke becomes erratic and a proper finish is impossible.

Bent Arm
Unless the arm is kept straight during the forward swing consistency and power are impossible and the stroke will tend to be erratic.

Insufficient Turn
Unless the shoulders are turned sideways at the preparation stage the racket cannot be taken far enough back and the body's weight cannot be carried forward into the stroke. The tendency, then, is to hit across the flight path of the ball instead of through it, which produces an erratic and often mis-hit shot.

Hitting the Ball off the Wrong Foot
Forehands hit off the right foot and backhands hit off the left foot do not allow the weight to be carried forward into the shot. Occasionally players get away with forehands hit from an open stance, but to do so the shoulders have to be turned more than usual and the whole stroke becomes somewhat static.

Taking the Ball Behind You
If you do not meet the ball until it has passed you it is again impossible to carry the body's weight forward into the shot. The player will tend to fall backwards off the shot and sky the ball unintentionally high.

Incorrect Grip
Unless the grip is correct the angle of the racket face will be wrong as it meets the ball and will impart unintentional slice or top spin to the shot.

Lifting the Head on Impact
This tends to pull the racket off its true path because the shoulders and arms pull up off the shot, following the head, again producing an erratic and often skied shot.

Not Watching the Ball

A difficult fault to spot but surprisingly common. It results in 'woolly' shots that are sometimes hit in the centre of the strings and timed properly and sometimes near the frame and timed badly.

Bad Footwork

Unless your feet carry you to the right place at the right time the whole stroke has to become a compromise: you are either too far away from the ball and reaching for it or too close and cramped for space to swing. In these cases the stroke appears awkward and out of balance.

Not Bending Knees for Low Balls

It is important to reduce the height of the swing's plane *only* by bending the knees. Otherwise the player reaches down from the waist and drops the head of the racket by loosening the wrist. The whole stroke is then chancy and sloppy.

Taking the Racket Back at the Wrong Height

This results in the forward path of the racket moving across the intended flight path of the ball instead of through it.

Preparing Late

Unless you get the racket back and the shoulders turned early the stroke inevitably deteriorates into a hurried wristy flick with consequent loss of control and accuracy. Beginners often try to swing the racket quickly, believing this will give them more pace on the shot. In fact they only produce erratic shots and would do better if they got the racket back early and let it do the work with a full, firm swing.

4. THE SERVICE

The service is the most important single stroke in tennis. It is the only stroke that can be made entirely at your own pace without interference from an opponent. Accordingly, whatever your standard, however poorly you may serve, remember the golden rule of serving – take your time. I am continually amazed to see players – sometimes even good players – rush up to the baseline to deliver a service without any apparent thought or preparation. When I am waiting to receive service in a match I am always delighted when I see my opponent rushing himself like this, because I know that his first serve will be erratic and he will serve many double faults.

The service is the one stroke that you can practise on your own while you are learning. Go out with 20 or 30 old balls and groove the swing. Remember it is up to all of us to make the best use of our physical capabilities. Obviously a tall person has a great height advantage and should aim to make his service a really formidable weapon. If, like me, you are short then practise even harder to make your services consistent and accurate. Accuracy makes up for many missing inches.

BASIC SERVICE

The Throwing Action
The whole basis of serving is to *throw the racket head at the ball with all the weight of the body behind it.* As the service is a throwing action it is as well to be sure that you can throw the ball from one end of the court to the other with reasonable power.

Picture a cricketer or baseball player throwing hard to the wicket keeper or baseman. He gathers the ball, tucks his right hand near his neck with his arm bent and wrist cocked and turns his shoulder sideways to the direction of his throw. The weight of the body is on his bent back leg and his left elbow is pointing up at 45 degrees – his whole appearance suggesting a coiled spring about to be released. As he throws the ball he straightens his right leg and pushes forward on to the left leg while turning his shoulders and trunk from the waist to face his target as the right arm speeds forward to deliver the ball with a final flick of the wrist to add the last extra ounce of power to the throw.

The action of serving in tennis is very similar, with the racket head being *thrown* at the ball. Once you are confident you can throw a ball properly pick up your racket, adjust your grip to the one you have decided to use for serving and move over to the baseline.

The Stance – Position of Readiness
For a service to the first court take up your position carefully about one foot to the right of centre of the baseline and stand evenly balanced with your feet a comfortable distance apart. The left foot should be brought up close to the line without touching it (it would be a foot fault if you did) and pointed at the far right-hand corner of the opposite baseline. Thus you will be standing half sideways to the direction of your intended service looking at the target slightly over your left shoulder.

For serving to the second court take up a similar position but with the left foot pointing towards the right-hand net post.

At this time the racket should be held firmly and be lightly in contact with the left hand at the shaft. The left hand should be holding two balls – the first between the thumb and first two fingers and the second kept on the palm by the last two fingers. (If your hand is too small to hold two balls comfortably then, as a temporary expedient, put one in your pocket and serve with one which should be held between the thumb and first two fingers.)

This is the position from which you will build up your service swing so prepare carefully and *take your time*. At this moment you should be thinking of the type of service you are going to deliver – perhaps a flat one down the middle. Make a mental picture of the exact spot you are aiming at – in this case the right hand corner of the service box next to the centre line.

THE FLAT SERVICE SWING

Preparation
The key to consistent serving is to have a consistent throw-up or 'place-up' as I prefer to call it. For the normal flat service the ball should be placed (never 'flicked') from a straight arm and braced wrist about one foot higher than you can reach with the racket. It should ideally be slightly to the right of the head and well forward, so that if it were allowed to bounce the ball would land about two feet inside the baseline opposite the right shoulder.

From the readiness position both arms drop down together until the left hand, keeping straight, moves upwards to *place* the ball in the air. At the same time the racket arm moves straight on past the legs to begin a full swing that will take it up behind you and level with the head before

The flat service, to be powerful and consistent, depends upon a sound technique to combine stance, throw-up, a rhythmical swing, and the throw of the racket head.

the arm starts to bend at the elbow to let the racket drop down in a deep arc behind your back.

As the arms start to move downwards the weight rocks back on to the right foot. As the arms start to swing upwards the weight moves firmly on to the left foot and the left leg begins to bend in preparation to launch the *throw*. You are now coiled like a spring ready to explode into the service throw – just like the cricketer and baseball player before their deliveries.

Execution

The racket is thrown up at the descending ball in a continuation of the circular swinging action. As the left leg straightens to launch the body's weight into the stroke, *the racket head makes contact with the ball at full stretch when the racket, arm, body and legs are in a straight line leaning forward into the court.* Correct timing of the place-up and swing are vital if full power is to be obtained. Also vital is the timing of the wrist action. To obtain full racket-head speed the wrist takes the racket through 180 degrees immediately before and after the hit while the arm moves forward approximately 18 inches.

Finish

After the blow the racket continues its downwards course outside the left leg while the weight comes through naturally on to the right leg some way inside the court. From this position it is easy to follow in fast towards the net or to check and maintain a baseline position.

For the sake of convenience I have broken the service up into its various phases. In fact, of course, *the service needs to be a continuous movement in which timing, rhythm and balance are unified in one harmonious and graceful action.* Once you have seen a player of the calibre of Pancho Gonzales, Stan Smith, or Lew Hoad in action you are unlikely to forget the beautiful, easy service power they can command. That sort of co-ordination takes years of practice but it is worth working for, because at least half the points of every singles match begin with your service, and the more outright winners you can produce the easier the game becomes.

While you are learning do plenty of practice swings in front of a mirror. If there is no room to use a racket go through the whole swing, including the throw-up, holding a rolled newspaper.

Although with other strokes I have confined my remarks to the basic shot I feel the service is so important that a word needs to be said about such variations as the slice and kick services.

THE SLICE SERVICE

The basic action is the same as for the flat service but the ball is placed-up much further to the right so that, if allowed to fall, it would bounce about 18 inches inside the baseline and 6 inches wide of the right shoulder.

The path of the racket takes it round the outside of the ball to impart sidespin and it 'brushes' the ball with an open face instead of meeting it with a full face as it did during the flat service. *It is important to retain a full wrist action which gives speed to the racket head, and to follow through strongly to maintain control of direction.*

The more spin that is imparted to the ball the greater its swerve from right to left, but the slower its trajectory. Accordingly, various degrees of spin are used depending upon the intention of the server. A commonly used serve, because of its relative consistency, is the fast serve down the middle line (from either court) with only a touch of slice for control. At the other extreme is the serve from the first court that carries heavy slice, bounces half way down the far left-hand service line and spins really wide to carry the opponent clear of the court opening up a huge gap for a volley or approach shot. This is especially useful on fast surfaces that exaggerate slice, like damp grass, wood or some of the synthetic carpets.

Lefthanders like Rod Laver, Roger Taylor, and Tony Roche use this heavy slice most effectively to the backhands of righthanded opponents in the second court.

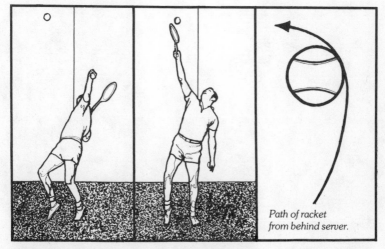

Path of racket from behind server.

The slice serve is a useful variant to carry the receiver wide of the sidelines. The ball must be thrown up further to the right and the racket head delivers a glancing blow.

THE KICK SERVICE

This is widely used as a second service in both singles and doubles as it is easy to control, can be hit hard and high over the net, and is difficult to return because it dips sharply in flight and kicks up high after bouncing.

The ball should be placed in the air above the left shoulder, not as far forward as for the flat and slice services so that, if it were allowed to drop, it would bounce opposite the left shoulder and about six inches inside the baseline.

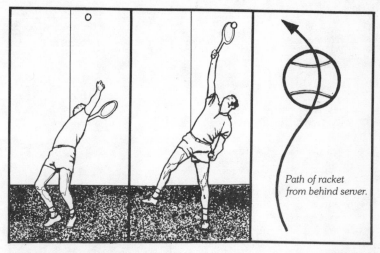

Path of racket from behind server.

For the kick service, the ball should be struck a little lower than for the flat serve, with the racket head 'brushing' the ball diagonally.

The ball is struck a little lower than for the flat serve allowing you to hit up at the ball. The path of the racket head takes it below the ball and 'brushes' diagonally up the back of it to finish above the top right-hand corner. Accordingly the back must be arched and the shoulders turned more than in the flat or slice services and the knees should bend more too. *Hit this service hard. It is by hitting lots of spin on the ball that control is achieved.*

Do not expect to master the spin and kick services over-night. It takes

Bjorn Borg about to launch himself from this beautifully arched position into a fierce throwing action as he hits up and over the ball on service.

many hours of patient practice to get accustomed to using the different angles of racket face. At first you will probably spray the balls all over the court, but do not worry – everyone begins that way, I know I did!

Practising the Service

There is an old saying in tennis that a player is as good as his second service. When you think about it this makes sense because even good servers rarely get more than 65 per cent of their first serves in. There are many players who can deliver a fast cannon ball for up to 65 per cent of the time but few who can still put pressure on an opponent by the pace, depth and accuracy of their second services.

Accordingly when you go out with that large box of old balls spend as much time practising the slice and kick services as you do the flat first service. Remember that depth is the quality that prevents an opponent from moving into the attack. The only time a service should be short is when you are using heavy slice or excessive kick to the sidelines to carry the opponent far out of court.

Ball boxes or other targets placed in the corners of the service courts are useful guides to accuracy. You will probably be surprised to find how difficult they are to hit, but grouping is the important thing with a high percentage of the services landing in the area of the target.

At a more advanced stage, when you feel you have mastered the actions, always serve in pairs to alternate courts, the first serve followed by the second. Also start to follow these practice serves to the net so that you develop the place-up far enough forward to carry you naturally into the court.

Finally, repeat this last exercise with a friend actually returning the serve (if he can!) so that you make the first volley. Unless you do this there is a danger of developing the service in isolation from the first volley so being slow off the mark, whereas the serve and volley together are an integral part of the regular pattern of your service games. If the player is as good as his second serve it is equally true that the service is as strong as the first volley.

COMMON SERVICE ERRORS

Incorrect Grip

Only the 'chopper' grip will enable you to get full wrist movement and proper use of spin.

The heart of John Newcombe's powerful service action. The place up is precise; his eyes are glued to the ball; the left leg is bent. The full swing will take the racket down behind his back in preparation for the throwing action.

Erratic Place-ups
Unless you throw up the ball in the right place you will be continually 'chasing' it, resulting in a compensation of the swing so that each service is slightly different. Consistently good serving is entirely dependent on a reliable place-up.

Not Throwing the Racket at the Ball
The 'push' servers and 'swing' servers are all too common – usually because of an incorrect grip. These methods lack power.

Ball Not Placed High Enough
This loses power and angle because the server is not at full height. Too often a beginner will hit his service from a semi-crouched position.

Ball Not Placed Far Enough Forward
Results in loss of power. You cannot launch your full weight into the shot unless the ball is placed well forward.

Not Watching the Ball
Surprisingly common – resulting in mis-hit shots that are not timed properly. Try to watch the ball right on to the strings.

Too Square to the Net
Results in body weight getting in too soon before the arm comes through. You must stand sideways to achieve the correct use of body weight.

5. THE VOLLEYS

The forehand and backhand volleys – where the ball is hit before it has bounced – are two of the most exciting shots in the game, both to watch and play. There are few sights more thrilling than a rapid exchange of crisp volleys between four good players in a men's doubles, and there is nothing more satisfying in a match than to anticipate the direction of an opponent's passing shot and move across to deliver a winning volley out of his reach.

During the speeding up of the entire game which I have witnessed over the past 20 years with services becoming better, the ball being taken earlier and hit harder and players being prepared to take risks by moving to the net on almost any shot in an effort to rush an opponent, the volleys have become essential weapons in the complete player's armoury. Nowadays this applies to girls too, for women's tennis is experiencing the same quickening process and young players of both sexes should be prepared to learn to volley from the beginning.

Volleys are punching strokes where the racket head is punched firmly forward to meet the ball.

FOREHAND VOLLEYS *(between hip and shoulder height)*

Preparation

When you realise that the ball is coming to the forehand side change to the 'chopper' grip and judge the height the ball will be when you want to meet it. *Keep the wrist firm and take the racket only a short way back at this height while turning the shoulders to the right, away from the net,* so that you are sideways to the oncoming ball. If you have to move to the ball take short, quick steps still keeping sideways to the net with the racket back.

Execution

Having carried yourself to the correct position step forward and across on to the left foot and *punch* the racket-head through the ball along the intended path of your volley. You should meet the ball well out in front of you so that the body's weight goes into the stroke and the racket face should be slightly 'open' to impart a little controlling backspin to the ball. *Keep the wrist firm throughout the entire stroke.*

Notice the straight arm and firm wrist as I meet this backhand volley well out in front of my right foot.

Finish

The racket stops abruptly shortly after making contact with the ball. Unlike the ground strokes there is no long follow-through. Control is obtained by timing the ball properly and meeting it out in front with a slightly 'open' face. *The whole stroke is a short, sharp punching action with an abbreviated take back, a sharp punch on impact and little follow-through.*

The complete forehand volley looks solid and safe even when the low ball makes it necessary to bend the knees. The punch is made with an open racket face.

BACKHAND VOLLEY *(between hip and shoulder height)*

Preparation
As for the forehand volley except that you will be turning your shoulders to the left away from the net and watching the oncoming ball over the right shoulder. *As you take the racket back be sure to keep the wrist firm.*

Execution
Step forward and across on to the right foot and *punch* the racket head through the ball along the intended path of your volley. Meet the ball well out in front of you so that the body's weight goes into the shot and keep the racket face slightly 'open' to impart a little controlling backspin to the ball.
Keep the wrist firm throughout the entire stroke.

Finish
As with the forehand volley the racket stops its forward motion shortly after the *punch* has been made.

Because most beginners find it harder to support the racket on the backhand side than the forehand they often find backhand volleys easier to master if they 'choke-up' on the grip by holding the racket higher up the handle. This should only be a temporary expedient until the wrist becomes stronger.

A firm wrist is vital to successful volleying so resist any temptation to 'flap' at the ball. *The racket must present a solid face to the ball if pace and accuracy are to be obtained.*

Low Volleys
If the wrist is to remain firm and solid on all volleys it follows that the head of the racket must remain level with or above the wrist. Accordingly, to hit low volleys the whole body must be lowered *by bending the knees*. Otherwise the low volleys could only be hit by relaxing the wrist and dropping the racket head which would result in erratic and risky shots. The *punch* should be less powerful with a higher trajectory on the ball.

DRIVE VOLLEYS
You will sometimes see good players hitting shoulder-high volleys with a much fuller swing than I have been describing. To get greater power they take the racket much further back (as for groundstrokes) and 'drive' the volley for a winner allowing the head of the racket to follow through. Do not confuse these shots with the normal 'punched' volley.

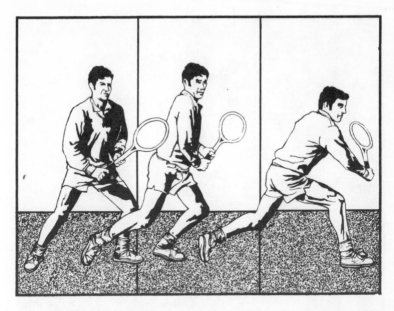

The ball should be met well out in front of the body on all volleys so that the racket head can be punched solidly through the ball with a firm wrist.

One of the brightest young Americans, Betsy Nagelsen, demonstrates a wonderful low volleying position as she crouches to punch the ball over the net during the 1974 BP Cup.

Practising Volleys

First of all see how far the ball rebounds off a firmly held racket without moving it. Then move the racket and arm forward to punch the ball. You will be amazed at the difference.

Do not start too close to the net when practising volleys – you should be about ten feet away while waiting for the ball to be hit to you. This encourages you to move forward quickly for each volley so meeting the ball well out in front of you, closer to the net. It is always easier to move forwards than backwards and also, of course, in a match your opponent will be less likely to beat you with a lob over your head – as he surely will do if he sees your nose almost hanging over the net.

Aim to establish control as well as power on your volleys. Remember that depth is essential on any volley that is not an outright winner, otherwise an opponent will have plenty of time to make a passing shot or lob.

Practise control by standing slightly to the left of the centre line, about ten feet from the net then moving in for forehand and backhand volleys directed to the left-hand corner of the court. Your opponent will know where the ball is coming and should be able to keep up a steady supply of volleys for you to hit. Repeat the practice to the right-hand corner standing now to the right of the centre line. The low volleys, of course, will have to be punched with less power than the hip-high ones and the ball will move in a higher arc.

An advanced form of practice involves both players (or even four players) volleying continually to one another. Aim to *punch* the ball right through him rather than wide of him – you are trying to speed up your reflexes rather than hit winners.

COMMON VOLLEYING ERRORS

Too Big a Swing
Control and timing are lost if the racket is 'swung' at the ball with a large backswing and full follow-through. Guide the racket by holding it lightly at the throat with the free hand. This helps you to turn your shoulder fully.

Loose Wrist
Unless the wrist is held firm the punch becomes a 'flap' with consequent loss of control. Some players try to use the wrist and arm to flick the ball over the net. This leads to inconsistency and does not take advantage of the pace of the ball coming towards them. Also timing has to be split-second perfect for a wristy volley to succeed.

Not Watching the Ball
Results in frequent mistiming and mis-hit shots. Try to see the ball meeting the strings.

Meeting the Ball Too Late
If the ball is allowed to travel level with your body or past it you cannot possibly step forward to meet it with a *punch*. Instead you will produce, at best, a defensive 'block' which has no pace and little control.

Shoulders Not Turned
By meeting the ball too square it is difficult to get power unless you have very strong wrists and arms. Advanced players have to be able to volley this way when there is no time to prepare normally, but beginners should concentrate on turning the shoulders fully and stepping forward on to the front foot.

Wrong Grip

Unless you use the neutral 'chopper' grip you will always have problems. By volleying with the same grips you use for ground-strokes you will have to change for your forehand and backhand volleys and, quite simply, there is not always time to do this. If you decide to use, say, the forehand drive grip for both volleys then the backhand volley will always suffer and *vice versa* with the forehand volley if you use the Eastern backhand grip for both volleys. However, if this is your method take heart; there are some leading players who are prepared to have a slightly weaker volley one side because the other one is so strong.

I have seen many great volleyers during my career – none greater than the Australian, Frank Sedgman. He was so fast of movement and reflex, so flexible and supple that he could *punch* volleys into the far corners from all parts of the court. The American, Budge Patty, had wonderful power and control on the forehand volley and Lew Hoad had a devastating backhand volley. Today Arthur Ashe and Jimmy Connors both have devastating volleys – especially off high balls which they murder with drive volleys of tremendous pace and power.

When I turned professional in 1957 I soon realised I would have to volley more than I used to as an amateur, if I were going to hold my own against Pancho Gonzales and Jack Kramer. It was a case of preventing them from dominating a match in the forecourt by getting to the net before they did. Fortunately I have always been able to see the ball early and move about the court quickly so that I became as happy at the net as at the back of the court.

I was never happier to get to the net quickly at a vital moment than during the all-important third set of that 1970 US final against Tony Roche. It was set-all and Tony had broken my serve in the eighth game of the third for 4-all to nullify my earlier 4-2 lead. Then games went with service until Tony led 6-5 and for the second time I was serving to save a set I should have already won. Then the worst happened. After two great returns from Tony and a missed volley I was 30/40 down – set point. Somehow I saved it and faced two more. It was saving the second one, I think, that finally won me the set because twice Tony's vicious passing shots should have beaten me, but somehow instinct saved me, as I lunged wide to a forehand volley and twisted back across the net for one on the backhand side that brought back deuce.

6. THE SMASH AND LOB

THE SMASH

The smash is an abbreviated form of the service with the same *throwing* action. It is an essential shot to develop otherwise an opponent will have an infallible answer to your volleying attempts – the lob. A good class player who smashes well will enjoy seeing an opponent send up a lob because it offers him the opportunity to smash a winner.

Preparation
The chief difficulty in smashing is to position yourself underneath the falling ball, and *correct positioning is essential to make a well balanced, powerful shot.*

As soon as you see the lob go up change to the service grip, turn sideways to the net with your left shoulder to the front and move beneath the ball. If you have to move back for a lob that would land behind you, maintain your sideways position and run back sideways with short, over-lapping skip steps.

If the lob is very high (even if it is short) let it bounce first and position yourself beneath it as it begins to fall again. This enables you to avoid attempting to smash a ball that is falling fast and vertically – no easy shot.

When you are in the correct position underneath the falling ball point your left hand directly up at the ball and take the racket behind the head and down the back in a shortened version of the serving takeback. Your weight should be leaning back over the right foot with the leg bent in the 'coiled spring' position ready to explode into the *throwing* action for the smash.

Execution
The throwing action of the smash is identical to the throw of the service and the only problem is to time the falling ball which is moving faster than your service place-up. If the lob is short maintain contact with the court with the back foot but for deep ones jump into the air off the back foot as you make the shot to get extra height and angle.

Finish
The follow-through of the racket is to the left of the body and should be

An abbreviated service swing gives the smash pace and consistency. The racket head is thrown at the ball after the player has moved into position.

a full one, exactly as in the service. The weight comes through on to the front foot.

Practising the Smash

Get an opponent to feed lobs for you to smash and do not be too ambitious at first. Build up confidence and the sense of positioning by dealing first with short lobs. As your skill develops get your opponent to mix short and deep lobs.

You will find it difficult to hit a smash when moving. If you are in mid-court and see a short lob coming go forward quickly so that you are stationary by the time the ball arrives. For the deep ones you will have to lean backwards as described and jump to make the smash. At the point of contact you will actually be 'leaning' slightly backwards in mid-air with the legs swinging forward to counter-balance your racket arm.

Do not neglect the lobs that arrive over your left shoulder – the most likely target for a good opponent. You must move quickly to the left, still in the sideways position, getting off the mark early with short skip steps to position yourself under the ball.

COMMON ERRORS WITH SMASHES

Incorrect Positioning

Unless you move quickly to get yourself *right under the falling ball* the racket swing has to compensate by moving out of its true throwing groove, resulting in an erratic and often mis-hit smash.

Not Turning Sideways

You cannot *throw* the racket head at the ball unless you are sideways to the direction of the lob. Remaining square will result in a pushed shot.

Lack of Attention

More than ordinary care must be taken to *watch the ball* which is falling fast and may be drifted out of its true path by the wind. As with every shot, failure to watch the ball properly results in woolly, mis-hit shots.

Overhitting the Ball

Remember that a winner can often be hit by placing the ball *in the right place at three-quarter pace.* If you try to over-hit you tend to disturb the whole rhythm and balance of the shot. Especially when the lob is deep hit a controlled smash to the base line and move in for the next shot.

mercial Union Mas ers

THE LOB

The lob is perhaps the most overlooked stroke in the game. So often the lob is thought of as a sign of weakness whereas in fact it plays a vital role in the armoury of every player – even the most attacking one.

There are three types of lob: the high defensive lob which is made as a deliberate tactical stroke; the defensive lob, often sliced, made when the ball is slammed at you so that you have no other choice; the fast low attacking lob, made usually with top-spin, which again is a tactical weapon.

At the top level of the game we play 'percentage' tennis which means that we try not to hit any given shot unless the odds of executing it successfully are in our favour. Accordingly there are many occasions in a match where an opponent has taken the initiative and forced us out of position when any reply but a lob would be a gamble.

These defensive lobs must be hit high and deep for two reasons: the longer the ball is in the air the more time you will have to recover position, and the high lob that falls almost vertically in the region of the baseline is the most difficult one to smash. The sliced defensive lobs, too, should be hit as high and as deep as possible, though sheer instinctive reaction will usually be your only chance when the ball comes at you so fast. The low topspin lobs are played most effectively when an opponent is moving forward. Rod Laver, Tony Roche, and Tom Okker use these lobs perfectly on the forehand side and many players today can hit them equally well on both wings including Ilie Nastase, Jimmy Connors, Bill Vilas, and Bjorn Borg.

Players brought up on slow courts like Andres Gimeno of Spain and Nicola Pietrangeli of Italy are masters of high lobs which are just as necessary and effective on fast courts. I remember once losing to Gimeno on the wooden court at Wembley in London chiefly because of his amazingly accurate lobbing. I also remember beating Art Larsen one year in the US Championships in an intriguing match during which both of us employed the lob most effectively so that by turns we were chasing back to the baseline to hoist another lob in reply.

Preparation

The preparation for lobs is identical to that for ground strokes (for indeed they are ground strokes) except that the racket head is taken back a shade lower.

John Newcombe has leapt to hit a crushing overhead in Boston in 1973. After hitting such a shot in the semi-final against Tom Okker he landed awkwardly and had to retire with a damaged left knee.

Execution

As with forehand and backhand drives – *keep the arm straight and the wrist firm* as you literally drive the ball into the air by starting below it and meeting the ball with the racket face square.

For the topspin lob the racket drops even lower on the take-back and is brought sharply up the back of the ball aided by a controlled movement of the wrist as the racket moves forwards and upwards.

Finish

The finish should be *above head height so that the ball stays on the face of the racket for as long as possible* to aid control.

Practising the Lob

It amazes me how few players bother to practise their lobs even though this is such a frequently used shot. Practise on both calm days and windy days so that you can experience any aiming-off to allow for the wind. Use targets in the corners of the baseline and get an opponent to hit balls wide of the sidelines so that you have to make the lobs on the run – as often happens in a game.

COMMON ERRORS ON THE LOB

Not Watching the Ball

It is all too easy to take your eye off the ball when an opponent is charging into the net. As usual this results in a mis-hit shot.

'Flicking' the Ball

Lobs, like ground strokes, must be hit with a firm wrist to result in a solid, dependable shot. 'Flicking' the racket at the ball, by using the wrist, results in erratic lobbing.

Not Following-through

Because some players are hesitant about lobbing (usually because they have not practised enough) they tend to stop the shot half-way. This results inevitably in short lobs that are easily killed.

The Wrong Lob

Do not try offensive topspin lobs in defensive situations. The percentage of success is not good enough.

Too Low or Too Short

Again, usually the result of insufficient practice. Err on the side of depth.

7. THE USES OF SPIN

*As your game begins to improve and you start to be more ambitious –
perhaps playing in club matches or in open tournaments – you will need
to know how to spin the ball to increase your range of shots and you will
also need to understand how to play against an opponent who spins the
ball against you.*

*Before explaining the principles involved in hitting topspin, slice and
side spin shots – the three principle spins used in tennis – I want to say
a word about orthodox and unorthodox players.*

A visit to Wimbledon, Forest Hills, or any other major tournament will
soon convince you that modern tennis has produced a multiplicity of
styles. There are players who stroke the ball, players who whip and lash
at the ball and even players who hold the racket with two hands. You
would think at first sight that there is no longer anything orthodox about
tennis, and I suppose the only orthodox thing nowadays is the natural-
ness of the champions' play.

Players like Tom Okker, Tony Roche, Ilie Nastase, Bjorn Borg,
Guillermo Vilas, and Rod Laver use a lot of topspin shots as attacking
weapons to make the ball dip at an opponent's feet when he comes to
the net or to bring the ball dipping down, with control, on passing shots
and even lobs. They also use spin to open up the angles of the court with
short cross-court forehands and short sliced backhands. All of them are
using their natural strength and suppleness of wrist to add a new dimension to their games. And this is what spin is all about – it is used to add
another dimension to the orthodox shots so that either extra pace or
extra control, or even disguise and surprise, is added to the basic
forehands and backhands and also to the volleys, lobs and drop shots.

Metal rackets have added another new dimension to the game. They
are easier to wield and so are well suited to the wristy players who like
to spin the ball. Also they impart greater pace and spin to the ball than
wooden rackets and so exaggerate the shots with topspin and slice.
Volleying against a player using a metal racket is a problem until you get
used to the extra pace and extra dip of the ball.

My own basic shots are more orthodox than the players I have just
mentioned and I rely on the basic principles – getting the racket back
early, carrying the racket head firmly through the ball in the direction of

my intended hit, and following through until the racket finishes high above my head to give me accurate and firm groundstrokes. I try to rely on consistency and accuracy and I generate extra pace, not by swinging faster at the ball, but by taking it earlier, soon after it has bounced.

TOPSPIN

How to Spin the Ball

First a word of warning. To be able to impart topspin to the ball you must be strong enough in the arm and the wrist to wield the racket easily, so be sure that the racket you use is not too heavy – especially in the head. Players like Tom Okker and even Lew Hoad, whose immense physical strength would surely allow him to use even a heavy racket, play with light-headed models.

Topspin, or forward spin, is achieved through letting the racket head drop below its normal level on the backswing of forehand and backhand drives. Then, as the ball comes off the top of the bounce and starts to fall, the racket is whipped sharply forwards and upwards across the path of the falling ball with a flexible wrist action that makes the ball spin forwards off the strings of the racket. The racket continues its upward and forward path and finishes high above the head as the wrist continues its rolling-over movement.

It is important that the racket should continue moving forwards during the stroke otherwise you tend merely to brush at the ball and lose the forward momentum so that the ball has little pace. Just watch the way Rod Laver hits a running topspin forehand to whip the ball past a volleyer. His forward momentum carries the racket forwards from way below the ball to high above his head as he whips his wrist through to give the ball its topspin.

On the backhand side Ilie Nastase has refined his topspin return of serve, even on fast courts, to whip the ball back past the advancing server, as I saw him do at Wembley in 1971 in the Embassy Championships when he beat Rod Laver in a marvellous five set final. He can flick at the ball almost like a table-tennis shot and disguise its direction either down the line or across the court. A shot like this does not happen overnight. Nastase, during the years I have seen him develop, has gradually learned to take the ball earlier and hit it more violently simply by experiment and experience. This is an important factor in adding any new shot to your repertoire. You must be prepared to experiment, even in match play, if you want to move a notch higher up the tennis ladder. Lew Hoad did this when adding his marvellous topspin backhand to the basic flat drive and safe slice that he already possessed. John Newcombe

This topspin forehand has carried Rod Laver's racket high above his head from a starting point well below the approaching ball.

had the same attitude when he added his topspin forehand lob. Years ago the shot was a rarity with him but nowadays I am never quite sure when I go to the net on his forehand side whether or not to expect that quick, low, spinning lob.

Manuel Santana brought a new shot to the game with his beautifully disguised topspin backhand lob. The racket was flicked up at the ball so late in its swing that it was a difficult shot to pick. There are many players now who can hit excellent topspin forehand lobs and these shots too, are both difficult to pick and difficult to hit because of the dipping trajectory of the ball. Rod Laver plays glorious topspin forehand lobs, sometimes when running flat out in a seemingly impossible position. It is this surprise element that gives Laver, Nastase, and Okker such an advantage – when the shots go in! Nowadays the younger players like Bill Vilas, Bjorn Borg, and Jimmy Connors hit with tremendous topspin on many of their shots. Borg and Connors have the added disguise of two handed shots on their backhands which make them difficult opponents to volley against.

One must recognise that, exciting though they are, these early-hit and heavily-topped shots – especially the lobs – carry a greater element of risk than the more orthodox flat-hit drives. The timing and flight of the ball have to be precise otherwise you give the point immediately to your opponent with an error, or mis-hit the ball, which gives an easy kill. Accordingly, developing players should be sure what they can achieve in the way of topspin by knowledge of themselves in practice. Only use the topspin shot at a time when you have a better than average chance of succeeding with it.

THE SLICE

It is safe to say that all players beyond the beginner stage often need to use slice on their drives. Slice is a basic requirement and is used in various situations of defence and attack. The greatest feature of slice is the degree of control that it gives to a shot. Even the most attacking players like the ones already mentioned, Laver, Nastase, Hoad, and Okker use a great number of sliced drives during the course of any match.

How to Hit Slice Shots

Slice is the opposite of topspin and imparts a backward spin on the ball so that it travels more slowly through the air than a flat shot and tends to hold in the air on its flight. When it bounces the ball tends to skid off the surface of the court and keep low, making it often a difficult ball for an opponent to hit if it has bounced near his baseline.

To impart slice to the ball take the racket back in a higher plane than for the normal flat drive. As you move forward to meet the ball bring the racket head, with an open face, down across the flight path of the oncoming ball so that the strings bite into the back of the ball to impart backspin. Let the racket head continue its downward and forward path after the hit for added control.

Unlike topspin shots you can impart slice to the ball without using any wrist action – though excessive slice can only be acquired by using the wrist. On my own backhand drive I impart backspin to the ball though my racket trajectory is almost flat. In fact it would not be strictly correct to say that my normal backhand drive is a slice shot – rather it is a flat drive hit with an open face which tends to impart the backspin to the ball and gives the shot its control.

From the back of the court, especially on slow European clay courts, sliced drives are commonly used to maintain the long rallies that one often sees in Europe. The ball can be hit safely high over the net and the backspin gives the ball control so that it drops inside the baseline. When the ball you are trying to hit has bounced high, say at shoulder level, a slice (or, of course, a lob) is the only way you can reasonably get the ball back. The high margin of safety which slice gives to ground strokes makes it an essential requirement for rallying when there is no pressure from an opponent, say from the net. Although it is more usually the backhand drive which players hit with slice, forehands too are often hit in this manner when rallying from the back of the court on slow surfaces.

As an offensive shot, the sliced drive has the advantage of being reasonably easy to hit early – soon after the ball has bounced and before it has reached the top of its trajectory. This is the shot you see players using when they are approaching the net from a short or mid-court ball. As they run forward they meet the ball well out in front of them with a block slice – a shot where the racket is brought down and through the ball with an abbreviated follow-through. This has the effect of digging the ball in when it bounces at the far end making it skid through low. The approach slice is a basic shot which Laver, Roche, Smith, and all the modern players use because it has a high margin of safety plus control so that you can get quickly to the net to set yourself for a volley.

When returning fast serves and high bounding serves the slice is an essential requirement. On the backhand side especially one has to be able to block through the ball with an open racket face with the racket gripped firmly.

In fact slice or backspin can be used in a variety of ways ranging from extreme defence, where the racket is brought right down across the flight path of the ball to send it high and safe to the far baseline, to direct attack where, as I have described already, the racket travels straight through the intended flight path of the ball with an open face to project it fast and low across the net – like my own backhand. In between these two extremes are any number of variations where basically the amount of spin put on the ball is in direct proportion to the safety factor one is intending to employ.

SIDE SPIN

There are two useful variants of slice which players often use on ground strokes to make the ball move sideways through the air, either to curl in towards the court or to swing away out towards the side lines.

Really they are variations or progressions of the sliced drives already described. The ball that is made to swing in from outside the side lines so that it eventually lands inside the court, is a variation of the slice where the racket head is taken round the outside of the ball on its forward path, in the same way that a slice serve is hit. Thus sideways spin is combined with the slice to make the ball move in a curving arc through the air.

The sidespin that takes the ball out towards the sideline is usually hit as a forehand approach shot. The racket travels across the ball from outside the body across in front of it so that again the ball carries sidespin combined with slice and moves through the air disconcertingly away from the opponent at the far end out towards the side line. Kramer was a master of this shot.

How to Play Against Spin

When you are at the back of the court you will know from the way your opponent has hit the ball whether to expect a flat drive, a topspin ball or a sliced shot. If your opponent's shot carries topspin you will expect the ball to bounce higher than for a flat drive, and accordingly you must decide either to step in and meet the ball soon after the bounce as it kicks up – probably using a blocked slice drive – or alternatively to move quickly backwards so that the ball bounces up, loses its spin and falls to a convenient height before you hit it back. Remember that topspin shots dip in the last part of their flight so that the ball will bounce shorter than a normal flat drive will.

When you see a slice shot coming to you at the baseline you must prepare early and expect the ball to come through faster and lower than normal, often with a skidding action on fast surfaces. Accordingly you should bend your knees a little bit more than usual so that you are down to meet the ball at the correct height.

In general you should always make solid shots against spin. Don't try and flick at the ball or let the fact that the ball is spinning put you off. On ground-strokes meet the ball firmly and grip the racket tight so that your own shot is a solid one which will cope with the spin on the ball.

The same, of course, applies when volleying against a spinning ball. Perhaps the most difficult shot to play is the volley against the heavily-topped passing shot that is dipping fast towards your feet. Watch the ball like a hawk, grip the racket firmly and get down low by bending the knees as you punch at the ball with your open racket face. If you meet the

Stan Smith about to play an approach slice as he starts to bring the racket head down across the path of the oncoming ball with an open face.

ball cleanly you should be able to hit a firm volley back across the net. Many players fail to make a good volley simply because they let the thought of what the ball might do as it comes towards them worry them. As with all aspects of tennis, practice against these spinning shots soon enables you to cope with them.

Against a heavily sliced drive, the ball will tend to drop off the racket face as you try to volley it and finish in the net. Accordingly, you should open the racket face a little more than usual and make your volley a really solid one with a firm wrist and a firm grip on the handle.

Undoubtedly the most difficult of shots to cope with is the fast topspin lob because the ball dips on its flight and makes it difficult for you to time the smash. This is a shot not practised often enough and I advise you to get a friend to go out and hit a succession of topspin lobs – no easy task in itself – so that you may get used to facing the dipping ball. Again, practice makes perfect, and the timing will soon come if you watch the ball really closely.

Finally, a word about drop shots and stop-volleys. I have said before that backspin or slice is used by players to control the ball so that those shots in the game which require the most delicate control and touch, namely drop-shots and stop-volleys, are both hit with backspin.

Drop-shots should be hit at a time when opponents are not expecting them, so don't overdo them or your opponents will soon pick them out and move forward, even as you are making the shot. You should aim to control the ball with backspin so that its trajectory makes it drop steeply just beyond the net and spin back off the court towards the net. Nicola Pietrangeli of Italy was a master of the drop shot. I have seen him spin the ball with such control that his shot has bounced over the net in his opponent's court and then bounced back across to his side of the net. This sort of shot requires delicate timing and much practice.

The stop-volley also should be used sparingly to create surprise and it, too, is a shot that requires delicacy of touch, timing and control. The ball is hit with backspin and travels only a short distance as it pops off the racket face across the net to die in the forecourt.

I believe that the development of tennis will bring an increasing use of spin – especially topspin. In an effort to hit the ball harder and earlier, players like Vilas and Borg are already tending to hit more and more topspin shots. They cannot hope to maintain a very high average of performance but at least spectators are in for a feast of excitement when they put it all together in a match.

8. THE VARIABLES

No two tennis matches are ever exactly alike. There are variable factors at work which affect the players in different degrees. The type of surface on which the match is being played, the type of ball they are using and the weather conditions prevailing at the time may all affect the outcome of a match – quite apart from the activities of the opponent, of course. Accordingly, one of the things a player has to learn is the way these variable factors will affect his own style of play and how he can turn them to his best advantage. Experience is the only teacher and, until a player has actually played on the various surfaces that are used for tennis, or tried to hit his shots with power and control using the many different makes and types of ball in existence, or has had to combat cold, rain, wind and slippery surfaces, he cannot really understand fully what the game is all about.

Although the notes that follow will tell you what to expect when meeting new conditions or situations, the only way of discovering whether your game fits those conditions – and if not what to do about it – is to go out and experience them for yourself.

In fact I always advise ambitious young players to experience as many different court surfaces, types of ball and styles of opponent as possible. Only then will they learn to play in all conditions.

COURT SURFACES

Basically there are five types of surface used in tennis. They are grass, loose-type hard courts, solid surface hard courts, permanent indoor courts, like wood, plastic tiles, or cork linoleum, and carpets which, of course, can be permanent but are more usually movable.

GRASS COURTS

Of the world's major championships, only Wimbledon and the Australian Championships are still played on grass courts. The US Championships used to be played on grass but so bad was its quality that a change to clay courts was made in 1975. As a surface grass is probably the least universal but, at its best, the most pleasant to play on. Perhaps this is a slightly biased view because I learnt my tennis on the grass courts of

In play against Jimmy Connors in the US Open Final 1974 – the last meeting at Forest Hills on grass courts. They have now been replaced by a type of porous hard court.

An early stage in my lengthy 1974 semi-final against Stan Smith on the matchless turf of Wimbledon's centre court. After losing the first two sets and facing a match point, I eventually won.

Sydney which are generally of a high standard. Obviously grass will become less important as maintenance costs rise and drive them out of existence.

A firm, dry grass court produces fast aggressive tennis where the big server and heavy volleyer are at an advantage. Unless the court surface is perfect – and there are all too few perfect grass courts in existence – the bounces are sometimes erratic, another factor which assists the heavy hitting, attacking player.

The ball skids through low and fast on a good court so that sliced shots are assisted by the natural reaction of the surface. Slice serves take an opponent wide of the side lines; slice approach shots skid through low and awkwardly and volleys hit with backspin slide away to the angles of the court. Accordingly, early preparation on ground strokes is essential because the ball comes through so fast. Also early preparation gives you a chance to adjust to a bad bounce. At the beginning of the season when the courts are fresh and green the balls tend to become heavy after a few games as they pick up the sap from the grass. This is something one adjusts to, allowing a little more height over the net and hitting with a little greater depth as they get heavier.

Movement is sometimes difficult, especially early in the season and footwear is therefore of paramount importance. I always use flexible, light shoes with a herringbone patterned sole which grips well. Grass enables you to slide into your shots and spoils the confidence of players who are used to a firm foothold.

The surface calls for forthright attacking shots and little finesse. Fast first serves, heavily sliced second serves and deep hard volleys win points.

LOOSE-TOPPED HARD COURTS

The clay courts of America and the 'terre battue' of France and Europe offer a complete contrast to grass. The ball digs into the loose surface, sits up and does not come through in the way that it does on grass. Because the bounce is slower the rallies tend to be longer and the technique different. Players brought up on these courts have longer, fuller backswings to their ground strokes and often have less aggressive services simply because the big server is handicapped by the slower bounce.

Matches played on these courts are good to watch because the players use every part of the court and fence for position rather like two chess players. The aggressive volleyer makes himself felt but he must approach the net behind sound attacking shots rather than gamble his way in as on grass.

An essential shot on these courts is the lob – too often neglected by the fast court experts but used with telling effect by such artists as Nicola Pietrangeli of Italy and Manuel Santana of Spain who each won the world's premier hard court event, the French Championships, twice.

These courts are frustrating to those players brought up on grass – just as grass is frustrating in its brevity to those continental players brought up on clay. Generations of young Australians have visited Paris for the first time and found the ball coming back once too often, point after point.

Most players, with experience, learn to enjoy matches on clay courts because every aspect of the game is brought into play and one has the satisfaction of creating situations that take some thought and patience instead of merely thumping out the points as on grass.

Again, footwear is of vital importance because, unless the court is kept well watered, these loose-top courts can become quite slippery. I find that the same shoes that I use on grass courts grip well on the clay courts too.

SOLID SURFACE HARD COURTS

Into this category fall the fast cement courts which are found in California, the slower Laycold courts which are all over America and the Tennis-quick courts which are spreading now all over the world as well as an assortment of tarmac and bitumen surfaces. Although the pace of the game varies according to the individual finish on each court this group all have one similarity. The footwork is much more positive and precise than on grass or clay courts. It is not possible to slide into your shots so that you have to be more precise in preparing for each shot to meet the ball comfortably. These courts have one great advantage over any other type – the bounce is always perfect (unless you count those odd occasions when the ball moves erratically off a join between two areas of the court). Accordingly this is an excellent type of surface on which to learn your tennis because your ground strokes become confidently grooved and the player is encouraged to go for his shots without having to worry about a possible irregular bounce.

Another plus factor for these courts is the perfect foothold which enables you to change direction quickly to cover all types of shot. It is thus fair both to the attacker and the defender and one does not have that stranded feeling at the net that you get on slippery clay or grass courts.

For players who are used to the lower bounce of grass or clay the high fast bounce of cement and the high slower bounce of Tennisquick take some getting used to. But most players come to accept and even to enjoy it.

Because of the jarring sensation and the non-give character of the surface (apart from Laycold) these courts are hard on the body. Legs and back quickly become sore with the constant jarring. For these courts the footwear needs to be different. Best are the thicker, smooth soled shoes readily obtainable in America which allow the foot to turn slightly on the surface of the court–unlike the patterned soles which grip too well.

INDOOR SURFACES – PERMANENT

There is a great variety of surfaces used for indoor play. To my mind nothing has yet improved upon wood as an ideal indoor tennis surface. The pace of wood when treated with paint to slow the ball a little is ideal – fast enough to encourage the attacker yet not too fast to prevent the

Bob Hewitt watches his partner Frew McMillan en route to their WCT doubles title in Montreal 1974. They are playing on Supreme Court–a synthetic carpet with a slow bounce.

defender from having a reasonable chance of success. The last wooden court at Wembley in London was an ideal pace and, to my mind, the carpet that was used there subsequently is not an improvement.

The plastic tiles found in Stockholm and other Scandinavian courts and the cork linoleum found in Germany are excellent in their way. The tiles tend to be rather abrasive and hard on shoes, balls, and even rackets if you are unlucky enough to scrape them on the court while the cork linoleum, with its slight give, is a pleasant surface to play on not unlike grass.

Generally speaking, attacking tennis pays off indoors on all three surfaces described because the bounce is true, enabling you to take the ball early, there is no wind to upset judgment and the foothold is perfect.

The footwear for these surfaces should be light flexible shoes with either a patterned sole or even a relatively smooth sole, both of which give a good grip and, in the case of the smooth ones, rather more turn on the surface.

THE CARPET COURTS

These are basically of two types – the PVC or rubberised surface like Uni-Turf and the woven surfaces (much like a real carpet) like Sportface or Nygrass. The plastic courts, laid in strips and joined by a solvent are slow and extremely punishing on the body. The bounce is high so that longer rallies develop giving increased spectator interest. Sheer physical strength becomes an advantage in playing on this type of court and someone like Rod Laver can cope with the high bounding balls and the sudden lunges to the side which are demanded on the plastic surfaces.

The Uni-Turf carpets can be used outdoors because they are unaffected by weather and the rain or snow merely has to be swept away before play begins. Uni-Turf has had the odd effect of altering the values of the game because of the way the ball bounces off it. Normally it is good practice to approach the net behind a drive deep to the far baseline. On Uni-Turf, however, such a shot sits up slowly and simply begs to be hit past the volleyer! Accordingly, a short approach shot, which would be suicide on grass or clay, becomes a good shot on Uni-Turf because the ball stops short and the opponent is forced to lunge forward to 'dig' it up – thus opening up the court for a volley past him. The same is true of volleys. Short ones pay off but deep ones, which on grass or clay are essential, merely ask to be hit. I can assure you that this readjustment of values takes some getting used to.

The woven carpets vary tremendously in pace. This is something which is affected by the type of surface on which they are laid. They tend to be faster on cement than when laid on wood. The Sportface carpet used more widely now in America is about as fast as I believe any court needs to be. At times it even seems too fast, and the spectators are robbed of some potential excitement.

The Nygrass carpet, I believe, has always been too fast. Also it does exaggerate the use of spin – especially slice – and the ball seems to continue on its path as if drawn by an unseen magnet.

Because of their holding effect on shoes both these carpets are excessively demanding physically and undoubtedly the smooth-soled shoe is the answer. Otherwise muscle strains, sprains and joint jarring will become all too common.

There is one other indoor surface that I should mention – the canvas court – which was the standard surface in my early days of professional tennis. We used to travel round with our own canvas court, putting it down on whatever surface happened to be there. Sometimes it went straight over an ice rink. At other times it went on the concrete floor of an exhibition hall or even the wood of a large dance hall. At all times it was fast. It used to be stretched by guy ropes attached to the surrounding area and sometimes there was not room to stretch it tight so that it even moved as you checked in full flight. It was an eerie sensation and one which Pancho Gonzales became supremely well adapted to. He used to love thundering down his mighty service and charging to the net in those arenas where often it was well nigh impossible to lob because of the low roof.

Undoubtedly we are still at the beginning of artificial indoor surfaces and I have no doubt that in the years to come we shall see others which give different characteristics. To my mind the ideal would be a medium pace court with perfect foothold that allowed a little movement and that was slightly yielding in the way that grass is. Whether or not the experts can come up with such a surface remains to be seen.

TYPES OF BALL

There are two types of tennis ball in general use – the conventional one which is pressurised to between ten and twelve pounds per square inch with either gas or air, and the pressureless variety which relies for its rebound entirely on a thicker inner core.

These latter balls tend to feel extremely heavy on the racket and make hard work of the game. At club level they are reasonably popular, but their lack of crispness and slightly dead feel make them generally un-popular with the leading players. They tend, too, to produce sore arms and shoulders as players try to hit harder and harder in an effort to get greater pace from this more sluggish type of ball.

Within the group of pressurised balls there is a tremendous range of performance brought about both by the type of cover employed and also by the liveliness of the rubber core.

As far as one can generalise, you find in America a much livelier, faster, higher bounding ball than you find in Europe or Australia. It is perhaps characteristic of Americans who like superlatives, for exciting and explosive shots are possible with their faster ball, which suits their temperaments. The same fast core is available in either regular covers or thicker, hairier 'heavy duty' covers which are designed to give greater end wear on abrasive surfaces.

With the slower pace of life in Europe it is appropriate that the slower balls allow the artistic games of their expert clay court players to flourish.

In Australia we have gone for the slower ball with the heavier, longer-wearing cover which makes for rallies even on our grass courts – especially early in the season when the courts are green and sappy, and also during night play under floodlights, when there is often a small amount of dew about which makes the surface of the balls damp and tends to fluff up the covers.

In countries which are at a high altitude like the 7500 ft of Mexico City, the 6000 ft of Johannesburg and the 5000 ft of Teheran, a special type of ball is used, known as the high altitude ball. This is made to a reduced compression and a lower bound to compensate for the thinner, rarer air in those places.

In England and Australia most of the tennis balls are sold in cardboard boxes so that their internal pressure will depend on their age – the length of time they have spent on the manufacturers' and retailers' shelves. With age they get softer because the internal pressure falls as the gas or air gradually diffuses through the core and cover.

For major championships, like Wimbledon, the balls are tested individually so that they are exactly the right pressure and hardness. But in clubs one sometimes finds the balls softer than they should be which gives greater control though less pace in play.

Throughout America, and in much of the rest of the world, tennis balls are sold in airtight tins. Accordingly they are at factory pressures and compressions when used. This makes them sometimes unplayably fast.

It is an interesting fact that all these balls, even the pressureless ones, conform to the rigid performance specifications laid down by the ILTF and it only goes to show how much latitude they allow. It is generally the cover which gives the most noticeable playing characteristics to a tennis ball. The tighter the cover the less air resistance there is and the faster the ball flies through the air. With a looser heavy duty cover that fluffs up with use there is more air resistance, greater control and a slower trajectory through the air.

Obviously the faster the ball off the racket and through the air the greater the advantage to the bigger hitters. In America they predominate whilst the slower ball in Europe has produced a multitude of excellent strokers and inventive artists who are at a loss to cope with the excessive pace they find in American balls.

WEATHER CONDITIONS

Of all the many variables a tennis player has to face, the most frustrating and troublesome is undoubtedly wind. Of the several places throughout the world which are notorious for windy conditions, perhaps worst of all is Port Elizabeth in South Africa. Here the prevailing winds are always fresh and often strong so that it is not unusual to see two players forced to twist and turn to make their shots as the wind plays diabolical tricks with the flight of the ball. In Sydney where I learned my tennis we often have strong winds, so that from the very first I was forced to come to terms with it – perhaps a blessing in disguise which at the time I certainly did not appreciate.

I find that playing with the wind behind me I like to shorten my back-swing and my follow-through on ground strokes and play for a greater margin of safety over the net and inside the lines. There is little point in being more ambitious than conditions allow so always try to play within yourself when having the wind behind you.

Into the wind it makes sense to lengthen your back-swing and have a full follow-through to get all the controlled power you can into your shots. This is the time to use those topspins and slices to make the ball behave awkwardly for your opponent.

Generally speaking, the rule for coming to the net with the wind is to use topspin to make the ball dip inside the court and against the wind to use slice so that the ball will die away in front of your opponent.

Try and forget how bad conditions are and, when in trouble, make it as awkward as possible for your opponent by hoisting lobs that swirl about. The fact is that there are very few occasions indeed when we play our matches in perfect conditions so that it makes sense to accept existing conditions and to try and make them work for you instead of becoming preoccupied with what is wrong with them. When the wind is blowing strongly across the court it makes sense to hit your passing shots down that side of the court where they will be blown in. When you go to the net yourself then cover that side of the court too and expect your opponent to hit them fairly wide.

The sun often proves the undoing of inexperienced players who let the glare worry them when they are playing at the sunny end. The sensible thing to do is not to come to the net against a very difficult sun unless you are sure of a very weak reply. If you are lobbed then let the ball bounce rather than risk a hazardous shot that you cannot really see. From the other end use the sun as a weapon and lob your opponent if you feel that he is not going to be able to see the ball to have a good shot at it. It is no more gamesmanship to use conditions in this way than it is to serve slice serves on courts that take a lot of spin.

On wet grass courts it often pays to hit the ball short to your opponent both on the drive and the volley. The ball will tend to die quickly and your opponent, scrambling forward, will be completely unable to recover for the next shot.

9. PSYCHOLOGY AND TACTICS

Tennis is essentially a thinking man's game. It begins before you get near the court. As with a dedicated professional in any walk of life, the tennis player should study all aspects of the problem. Just as a doctor will look at the case history of his patient and then give him a thorough examination before proposing a course of treatment, the tennis player should make a careful study of his future opponent, then think about the tactics he should adopt before venturing out to the match court.

It is not uncommon to see the world's great players like Rod Laver, Stan Smith or Arthur Ashe sitting quietly watching the early rounds of the tournaments in which they play. You might suppose that they were good enough not to need to look at the way lesser players hit the ball – but that is the first lesson to learn. The reason these players are as good as they are is that they take careful note of all the players they are likely to meet including fast-improving juniors. In other words, they are thoroughly professional in their preparation.

Whenever I watch a player I try to read his game and, more important, his mind, to try to understand what shots he likes to play, what shots he finds more difficult and how he reacts to the stresses of a match. I also watch his movement because it is surprising how some players who cover the baseline at tremendous speed are quite slow moving forward to the short balls.

It is vital for success to be in the right frame of mind to play a match. Your attitude to a particular match will, in part, depend upon the degree of preparation you have made for it. It takes a tremendous amount of hard work and a lot of thought to become a good player and the talented youngsters who fail to make the grade more often fail mentally than physically.

During the match itself you have two things to consider – your own game, that is the way you are hitting the ball, plus your tactics and also the game your opponent is playing. Is he playing the sort of game you expected, having made a study of him, or is he trying something new? Only experience will teach you how to strike the right balance between continuing with your normal game and adapting your own shots and tactics to defeat your opponent.

Experience teaches you that players have favourite surfaces, usually because their style of shot and even their grip on the racket is governed by the surface on which they learnt to play. For example, the great American Champion, Tony Trabert, learnt his game on the slow courts in mid-west America. He had a pronounced grip change from forehand to backhand made possible by the relatively slow bounce of the ball. He hit his backhand with the thumb down the back of the handle and a fine, solid shot it was. Trabert started with a low take back and finished high on the follow-through, thus imparting topspin to the ball. He could hit this shot early and had great confidence in it. But on fast surfaces like grass, where the ball came through fast and low, he found it sometimes difficult to prepare early on that side to get into the hitting position. Accordingly, players who could switch their attack from his forehand to his backhand side with early taken fast balls that were deep (and it took an extremely high class player to do it) could embarrass him as he was not able to prepare early enough.

During my first years as a professional in the mid 1950s, some of the players began to use lighter rackets because the pace at which the game was being played did not allow them time to get their rackets into position early enough to make solid and consistent shots. Pancho Gonzales, for instance, went to lighter rackets indoors on fast courts. He would have some lead tape in his luggage with which he used to weight up the racket when he played out of doors. He was constantly experimenting, juggling with the weight and balance to get exactly the right sort of weapon that he needed for the conditions.

Frank Sedgman and Lew Hoad both went to lighter rackets as more and more indoor events came into the calendar. Today Rod Laver is constantly altering the size of the handle of his racket with surgical tape that he applies to the wood before wrapping on the leather grip. He says that if he finds he is hitting the ball longer than he wants to, then he reduces the size of his grip. This seems to give him greater facility for topspin which brings the ball down quicker and so reduces the length of his drives. Conversely if he is netting too many balls then he will increase the size of his grip to lengthen his shots. It is the knowledge gained from long experience, plus a dedicated professional approach, that takes account of even the tiniest details of preparation that sorts out the champions from the rest.

Some players like to play to the same regular pattern and never change, regardless of their success or failure. These unthinking players are comparatively easy to play against – not because they are bad hitters of the ball but because inevitably they are limited. Provided that you

Arthur Ashe's powerful, uncompromising game poses special problems. Rallies are few and there is no time to develop your rhythm so accuracy and depth are essential on returns and groundstrokes.

have the skill then you always know where the ball will be directed in a certain situation.

All players have their own rhythms. Some like to play fast, like Tony Roche, who likes nothing better than to hustle between points when serving. Others play at a more even pace as I do myself. I hate to rush, but too long a delay between points tends to disturb my concentration. Some players, like John Newcombe, have a slower and more deliberate pace which suits them. Only by understanding the pace at which your opponent likes to play through studying his matches, will you know what to expect from him. It is senseless to fret about a player who you think is trying to rush you or about somebody whom you swear is stalling. Accept that this is their rhythm and try to keep to yours. On your service games you are the one who can dictate the pace and on your opponent's service games you should only be wary of being rushed. Never receive service until you are ready and, if your opponent's gap between first and second service is too short, then hold up your hand until you are ready to receive the second ball.

This brings us to an area of the game that often causes trouble and sometimes bitterness. I refer to gamesmanship. Undoubtedly there are players who are prepared to use unfair means to upset an opponent's concentration. We have all seen those shoe laces which have mysteriously needed to be tied between an opponent's first and second serve or those glasses which have needed extensive wiping and cleaning before an opponent is about to serve at 30-40 and 5-5 in the final set. Or worse, those occasions in matches without an umpire when the ball is called out when it has clearly landed in.

But there are more subtle cases of gamesmanship which are much more difficult to counter and much more difficult to detect. There have been players for instance who, at the change-over, start to compliment you on the excellence of your forehand on that particular day. They tell you that they have never seen you hit it better and simply marvel at its excellence. Before you know what has happened you are thinking so much about why your forehand is so good that you cannot hit one near the court. Then there are those players, who, like the rugby player who looses a blow at an opponent on the blind side of the scrum away from the referee's gaze, will deliberately foot fault if they know that there is unlikely to be any call from the umpire or, of course, if there is no umpire at all on their match. This form of cheating is much more difficult to counter.

There is then, a very fine dividing line between good, hard, tough match play and gamesmanship and none of the champions I have already referred to, Laver, Hoad, Newcombe, Ashe, and the rest, tough competitors all, would ever descend to such antics of gamesmanship.

Another class of court behaviour can have an equally devastating effect on an opponent even though it is not deliberately intended to produce that result. The temperamental outbursts of certain players, while appearing to upset them – as a result of a doubtful call or perhaps an intrusion from a spectator – have the effect of breaking the concentration of an opponent. I have suffered myself in this respect at the hands of Pancho Gonzales whose outstandingly competitive nature made it difficult, if not impossible, for him to stomach the inadequacies of some umpires and linesmen. While Pancho would never deliberately upset an opponent the effect on me was sometimes to disturb my concentration.

In the 1972 US Open final Arthur Ashe was clearly suffering from this in the vital period of the fifth set when Ilie Nastase gave vent to some outbursts which interrupted the course of the match. Again Ilie is the last person who would knowingly upset an opponent but he sometimes selfishly forgets that his own behaviour could affect others.

The psychological advantage of playing on home courts in front of a patriotic crowd is another factor which lifts certain players. In Germany, Wilhelm Bungert becomes inspired by the urgings of the German spectators; in Spain the national hero Manuel Santana would often perform miracles of artistry through the encouragement of his excitable countrymen; in Barcelona Juan Gisbert created a legend of invincibility in Davis Cup ties that was only shattered in 1972 by the Americans; in Milan the famous spider of the centre court, Fausto Gardini, had an unbeaten record in Davis Cup matches and used to encourage the demonstrative crowd, rather like an orchestral conductor, urging them to ever higher peaks of patriotic fervour.

That historic 1972 Davis Cup tie in Bucharest illustrates too, the effect that over-enthusiasm can have. Far from being inspired to peak performance, poor Ilie Nastase found the sheer weight of national expectation too heavy a burden to carry. His beautiful game fell around him in pieces under the determined onslaught of Smith. The psychological factor in this win by Smith was significant indeed.

To summarise then, the central factor in any tennis player's mental armoury must be concentration. Without it – and I mean the sort of deep concentration which can exclude any other extraneous thoughts from the mind except the job in hand – a player cannot control anything else. You cannot successfully change your tactics or impose your game properly upon an opponent unless you are utterly aware through every second of the match what is going on. This is perhaps the hardest of all attributes to acquire and those who are blessed with this are indeed fortunate.

A belief in your ability and a knowledge, through experience, of how to apply it to the particular opponent you are facing completes the psychological picture. For those players who lose confidence for a spell, which is perhaps the most distressing problem for a player to meet, you can only face up to the situation. Try to see clearly what is going wrong and get out on the practice court and seek to eradicate the weakness. A knowledge that everything possible has been done – which, of course, includes complete fitness, proper preparation and all the other things we have talked about – should restore the confidence without which it is impossible to wage psychological warfare.

Finally, a word of advice which I have gained from many years of experience. The consistent players (and I put myself in that category) are usually able to hold on to confidence and concentration more easily than the hit-and-miss type of players. The mental discipline necessary to play a consistent game both creates a mental attitude that breeds confidence in yourself and exerts mental pressures on an opponent who begins to wonder if he is ever going to be given a cheap point. That is why, in the search for perfection, I like to advise young players that control before speed makes good sense.

SINGLES TACTICS

Always try to study a future opponent when he is playing an important match. Don't watch the ball, watch him, and see how he reacts to the various types of shots his opponent gives him. In a close match does he tighten up on important points? If so, you need never be too nervous yourself when you get to an important point in the match. Where does he like to hit his passing shots, down the line, across the court, or does he lob a lot? Is he a good volleyer and does he take every opportunity to come to the net on short balls? Where does he like to volley – back to the place where the ball has come from or into the open space? Where does he like to serve – to an opponent's forehand or backhand or does he, perhaps, vary it as he should? How deep is his serve? Is there an opportunity to attack the second serve and get to the net yourself? Does he press home his own winning leads or does he falter when ahead? Does he fight when he is behind? Does he get upset by apparently bad calls? Does he try to influence the umpire – by walking across after a close first serve perhaps? Does he have any glaring weakness in his shots or is he good all round? Does he hit his passing shots high over the net or low? Does he ever try a drop shot or hit stop-volleys? Has he any imagination or does he play a stereotyped game? Does he hit the ball hard, or take it early to move an opponent about?

The answers to these and many other questions will tell you a great deal about your future opponent and give you an opportunity to decide on a plan of campaign. Work one out and try to follow it when the match begins. Change it only if you are incapable of carrying it out or if your opponent is mastering it.

I well remember the advice which Ken McGregor gave me when I was due to play the American Davis Cup player Vic Seixas at my first Forest Hills in 1952. I was 17 and had never seen Seixas play but Ken told me that if I went to the net against his backhand he would probably go down the line – his favourite passing shot. True enough he usually did and I won a lot of points by 'anticipating' on my forehand volley. Half the value of a plan, of course, is to have something positive to think about.

Try always to keep an opponent guessing. Give him shots you know he dislikes but not too often – unless, of course, his weakness is such that it is likely to collapse totally if you play on it.

In the WCT Dallas finals in 1973 Stan Smith was almost unplayable. Here he has caught Rod Laver in no-man's land near the centre of the court, and has punched the ball into the gap.

Vary your service in direction, pace and type – some flat ones, some slices, some kickers. Never let your opponent get set so that he knows what is coming next. The service is by far the most important shot in tennis. After all half the points of every match begin with your service. Try stretching your opponent wide, then serve at him. Try to do this by disguising the direction of your hit by adjusting your wrist at the last moment of the service throwing action. This is what the good players do. Someone like Stan Smith, Colin Dibley, or John Alexander can project a whistling ace down the centre line and, with a last minute adjustment of the wrist, can hit the same-looking serve wide to the sidelines. A consistent throw-up is vital to produce serves like this, so do spend plenty of time practising that throw-up.

If you are someone learning to play matches face the fact that there will be occasions when your opponent is simply too good for you. However good a match player you are and however competitive by nature, it is senseless to fret unnecessarily and upset yourself because you are losing to a better player. It is never a disgrace to lose in such circumstances and all you can expect to do is to fight for every point, run until you drop, and concentrate until the last point is played.

If you find you are losing try to decide why. If you are losing the points because your tactics are wrong then change them. If it is simply because your opponent's shots make it impossible for you to carry out the right tactics then try to appreciate the fact that you need to improve. Perhaps a little more pace on your own shots will give your opponent less time to make his and unbalance him – you can achieve this either by hitting the ball harder or taking it earlier. Experience will teach you what to do.

If you are winning then keep on with the same tactics – something you might think, that need not be said. But it amazes me how often I see even good players change a winning game and then wonder later why they lost.

Assuming, of course, that you have practised your strokes so that they are not letting you down and that you have trained hard so that you are as fit and as fast as you can be for your age or stage of development, then concentration is the biggest single factor that distinguishes good players from bad.

Concentration is something which some people have more naturally than others but which everyone can improve. Unless concentration is complete you will find yourself either presenting your opponent with points through simple errors or allowing him to take the initiative from you. You would be amazed how often a set is won from 2-5 behind so never give up and, whatever the score, concentrate deeply and try hard for every point.

Scramble after even the most hopeless looking ball because often in a close match it is the ability to scramble a few 'lucky' shots that makes the difference between winning and losing.

Remember, too, that your opponent has feelings. If the match is tight, he is suffering whether he is showing it or not. Some players play their matches in mental isolation from their opponents, not realising that they too are on the point of exhaustion or capitulation or frustration – or whatever. Stay in there and allow your opponent to crack first.

One final word about general elementary tactics. Something I have always tried to do in my matches – and it has paid handsome dividends – is to get my opponent's service back somehow to make him play the next shot. The pressure that builds in the server's mind when he knows, or rather believes, that he is going to have to play another shot at least to win the point is tremendous. You know when you are serving yourself how encouraging it is to win a service game to love with four errors from your opponent. Why give him the pleasure of such a luxury when he is serving – no one can really afford to be that generous. I suppose I am lucky to have quick reflexes which allow me to stand in quite close to return the ball. But, wherever you stand, try to hit your service returns by meeting the ball out in front of you and carrying the racket firmly through the ball in the direction of your intended return. That is better than making wild swings at the ball.

DOUBLES TACTICS

All players are different. Some excel as singles players and yet never shine at doubles. Others are equally happy at either version of the game and some players seem suited by their temperaments to be doubles specialists.

Such a man was Australian John Bromwich who used a very light racket, weighing about 12 oz, with a pencil-thin handle and strung very slack indeed. He hit a two-handed shot on his right side and a lefthanded forehand, but he served with his right hand. Like other doubles specialists Bromwich seemed to enjoy the rapid exchanges that doubles bring and enjoyed sharing the danger and the glory with someone he could talk to on the court. So good was his touch and so keen his appreciation of the angles of the court and the tactical manoeuvres required that all his partners were made to look spectacular. He would create the openings and his partner would finish off the set-ups he had created. When people ask me which pair I consider to be the best doubles players of all time I reply, half in jest, 'Bromwich and anyone'.

He and Adrian Quist were one of the best pairs I ever saw. Together they won no less than eight Australian doubles titles between 1938 and 1950 and then, long after their best days which coincided with the war, came back to win the doubles title at Wimbledon in 1950 – two years after Bromwich had first won that title playing with the young Frank Sedgman. Everyone who saw that earlier final marvelled at the way Bromwich nursed the 19-year-old Sedgman through a thrilling four set match against the Americans, Tom Brown and Gardner Mulloy, 5-7 7-5 7-5 9-7.

During my career there have been four other memorable Australian doubles pairs besides Bromwich and Quist – Frank Sedgman and Ken McGregor, who ruled the world in the early 1950s, Rex Hartwig and Mervyn Rose who won Wimbledon together in 1954, Hartwig and Lew Hoad, who won Wimbledon the following year and played Davis Cup Doubles for Australia, and the present world professional leaders, John Newcombe and Tony Roche who have already won five Wimbledon doubles titles. Perhaps I should add that Lew Hoad and I played well together at times – we won Wimbledon twice, but never really played much together as professionals because in the early days our tours did not coincide and later Lew's back trouble forced him to withdraw from the game for quite some time.

It came as something of a shock to realise that Rod Laver's doubles victory at Wimbledon in 1971 with his great friend Roy Emerson, was his first men's doubles title there. It was Roy's third men's doubles title in five final round appearances. This fact confirms my earlier remark about certain players being more temperamentally suited to doubles for, in Laver's case, no one could possibly deny his singles genius but somehow he has never been as happy playing doubles.

In doubles play the net is the vital area and the successful pair will be the one which commands the forecourt. After serving the server should always follow his delivery in and the returner should also attempt to make for the net as he drives the ball to the server's feet. This leads to some spectacular volleying exchanges at close quarters.

It is essential to be aggressive in outlook. A good lob must be followed to the net because this is a way of dispossessing your opponents of that vital area. If you are lobbed try never to let the ball bounce but take the ball as a smash and make for the forecourt once again.

If the service is the most important shot in singles then the service return is probably the most important shot in doubles – together, of course, with the server's first volley. This is the moment – right at the beginning of every rally where the point is most often decided. A good

Fred Stolle and I won the French doubles together in 1968, but here at Wimbledon we lost in the Final to John Newcombe and Tony Roche in five sets and were runners-up again to the same pair two years later.

return dipping to the server's feet will often allow the server's partner to move across for an interception on the volley. Good pairs create these interception opportunities frequently and are constantly criss-crossing, covering one another as the partner darts across to make a spectacular kill. As a protection against this treatment, the server should aim to place the ball really deep in an attempt to prevent an attacking return.

Accordingly the service in doubles is often hit below full power with a little extra controlling spin, both to be sure that it goes in and also to control the depth of it. As a returner of the serve it is important to keep your opponents guessing – drive some with topspin, take others early and chip them to the server's feet, lob some over the server's partner and some over the server himself and occasionally hit a full-blooded drive down the tramlines past the server's partner. Always deal summarily with weak, short second serves – run round and hit them fiercely on the forehand to the feet of the server as he runs in. If your opponents insist on hanging their noses over the net, then lob them and rob them of the net position.

The tandem formation, where the server's partner crouches down at the net standing just beside the centre line on the same side as the server, is a useful variant against a player who has got into a groove on his

Lew Hod and Rex Hartwig winning Wimbledon together in 1955 against me and Neale Fraser, the present Davis Cup captain. The previous year Hartwig had won with left-hander Mervyn Rose, and the following year Lew and I were successful.

Raul Raminez (Mexico) watches partner Andrew Pattison (Rhodesia) volleying to the second seeds in the Rome Final 1974, Juan Gisbert (Spain) and Ilie Nastase (Rumania). The unseeded pair scored an upset victory in straight sets.

returns. It is especially useful against the left-hander in the left court – that is if the server can be certain to place the serve down the centre line on the left hander's backhand which is generally weaker than his forehand.

Another useful variant is to have your partner back on the baseline with you as you return the serve – this when you are both having problems in making attacking returns. This tactic cuts out the drive-volley at your partner who would normally be standing in the centre of his service square when you are returning.

The tandem formation was one of the chief reasons for an American doubles victory in the Davis Cup challenge round in Brisbane in 1958. The story goes that Pancho Gonzales, coach to the American team, sent a message to the American captain Perry T. Jones who was sitting on the court, that the American pair Alex Olmedo and Ham Richardson should use the tandem formation when serving against Neale Fraser, the left-handed Australian (who was to win Wimbledon in 1960) playing with Mal Anderson in that Davis Cup match. The Gonzales message reached the court part-way through the third set after the Americans had lost the opening two sets 10-12 3-6. The new tactic completely destroyed Fraser's service return so that the Americans finally triumphed, 16-14 6-3 7-5 in an 82-game match – one of the longest in Davis Cup history – that clinched the tie 3-2 for the United States.

Besides being fun to watch, doubles is enormous fun to play. Without being subjected to quite the same lonely pressures as in a singles match, one can often get greater enjoyment out of the quick fire, quick thinking, thrust and counter-thrust of a good men's doubles.

There are four golden rules which apply to all matches.

1 Always try to win by playing your own game and imposing it upon your opponent whether you are a big hitting player or, like I am, someone who relies on accuracy and consistency. Try to play your own way.

2 Always play within yourself and don't try and attempt more than you know you can achieve with reasonable chances of success.

3 Play against your opponent's shots, not his name or reputation. Remember he has to hit the ball over the net and into the court to beat you so don't do the job for him by anticipating more than is really there.

4 Play within the limitations of the conditions you face in each match – the court surface, the speed of ball you are using, the weather conditions and, not least, your own ability.

Successful match play depends upon knowing your strengths and weaknesses and making the best use of them.

Let me now tell you about one of my own matches which called for all the qualities of match play, psychology, and tactics that we have been talking about.

10. THE DREAM FULFILLED

It was high noon in Texas on a bright afternoon in mid-November. Everyone stood to attention with heads respectfully bowed as the tinny notes of 'God Save the Queen' blared from the loudspeakers of the amphitheatre. I felt the tingle of excitement that always grips me as the trumpets reach their crescendo. Before anyone had had time to move, the vibrant notes of 'The Star Spangled Banner' froze the scene once again.

I raised my head slightly and allowed my eyes to take in the scene. Immediately opposite me, standing three yards beyond the centre service line to balance my own position, was Rod Laver, resplendent in matching gold shirt, shorts, and socks. Beyond him and slightly to the left on the far tramline stood four ball boys, two each side of the two-man colour party proudly holding 'Old Glory'. Behind me a pair of soldiers honoured the Union Jack.

Without raising my head I could see to my left the blue-robed figure of Janice Bain who, as Miss Texas, led the singing of the national anthem from her position facing the net some ten feet behind the 'T' of the service square. On her right stood Tony Trabert, the referee for the match, and on her left was Don Mordecai, the match manager. Beyond her, drawn up in two lines from each corner of the base line, were the 12 court officials.

My eyes moved back and momentarily exchanged a glance with Rod, who raised his eyebrows to signify his awareness of the tension we both felt. Looking beyond him again I saw the low line of the rich blue plush drapes that divided the court area from the spectators and, beyond the court, seats rising to the dim area of the roof with the multi-coloured tiers of spectators.

Glancing now to the left I could see the red, white, and blue bunting adorning the high wall of the Municipal Auditorium, Dallas, and beneath the line of its scalloped edge the large names of the 20 cities which had staged the legs of the 1971 World Championship of Tennis – Washington, Louisville, Rome, Teheran, Cologne, Toronto. . . .

Further to the left, in the official seats above the nine-foot blue drapes, stood the man whose dream was being turned into reality. Lamar Hunt had drawn upon his experience with the Kansas City Chiefs, one of the top American professional football teams, and other sporting ventures in basketball and soccer in an effort to create, in his own words, 'the most successful competition in professional sport that is, at the same time, an artistic success'.

The 8200 spectators who stood waiting for the anthem to end were here to watch history being made. This was the final of the first World Championship of Tennis, a tournament between the eight men who had led on points at the end of the year-long 20-tournament tour. It was a match which carried a world record first prize of $50,000, and the winner would also receive a sports car and a suitably inscribed diamond ring.

The last notes of music died away to be replaced by a spontaneous burst of applause for Neil Armstrong as he stepped forward to be presented to those of us who were on the court. As I shook his hand I could not help wondering what he really felt as his foot had taken that first historic step from the last rung of the lunar ladder. If that had been a giant step for mankind, then his presence here at today's final marked it as a giant step forward in professional tennis. For Rod and me it was a moving experience to be taking part, for we had both been through the years of struggle in professional tennis when our stage had often been a poorly lit, half empty hall, where the canvas court was loose because there was not enough room at the side to stretch the guy-ropes tight, and where the low rafters made it impossible to lob.

Jack Starr of New York, who was our umpire, called us over to the chair and gave Neil Armstrong a racket to spin for us. Rod won the toss and said he would serve. I took a deep breath and walked back to begin the warm-up. As I did so it occurred to me that this was the second world record prize money final I had contested in 14 months. The previous year at Forest Hills I had been fortunate enough to win the US Open with its first prize of $20,000, and I hoped this might prove a happy omen for today. Being honest with myself I realised that it most probably would not, because Rod had been in tremendous form lately and my recent record against him was not encouraging. I knew that today, besides needing the lucky breaks, I would also need to call upon all the reserves of skill and experience that I had acquired from a lifetime's association with the game. Twenty-five years of competitive play had taught me that the man behind the racket is the real adversary – not the shots he plays. When all else is equal, it is the character of your opponent you must overcome and no-one, I knew, was harder to overcome than Rod Laver.

I thought about the impressive build-up for the final. The timing was right – the match was scheduled for November 26 – the day after Thanksgiving Day which is a national holiday. Rod and I spent much of our time appearing on television and radio programmes or being interviewed by the Press. On the Tuesday night, WCT staged a magnificent banquet at the Fairmont Hotel, to which everyone who had been connected in any way with the tour had been invited, in addition to many of the world's tennis writers and one of the world's great tennis fans, Charlton Heston.

Lamar Hunt had called upon the expert services of his promotion team from Kansas City Chiefs to produce a colour film outlining the whole 20-tournament tour and highlighting the quarter-finals and semi-finals in Houston. At an appropriate moment the lights dimmed and the curtains which had been decorating one entire wall drew back to reveal three screens. On the centre one the film I have described appeared and on the outer two a series of colour slides depicting scenes to illustrate the action that was taking place on the screen between them – a fantastic production which drew lengthy applause.

On a raised plinth and glittering in the illumination of a lone spotlight stood the gold trophy we would be playing for, which had formerly been the Kramer Cup, the trophy offered for a team competition between the professionals which had been organised along the lines of the Davis Cup. I knew it well because ever since it had last been contested some years previously it had rested on a table in our living room at home.

Then came the speeches. It was embarrassing to sit listening to Rex Bellamy of the London *Times* describing my part in the growth of tennis and Rod must have felt equally embarrassed as Bud Collins of the Boston *Globe* painted a verbal picture of his great career. Charlton Heston paid a moving tribute to the game which, he said, gave him and millions like him so much enjoyment both as spectators and competitors. Michael Davies, the Executive Director of WCT said simply and graciously how proud everyone concerned with WCT was that the venture had proved so successful. Characteristically, Lamar Hunt remained modestly in the background.

Even Jack Jones, who was appearing in cabaret at the Fairmont, became involved in the proceedings and one afternoon he appeared in the lobby of the hotel dressed in his tennis clothes, inspired, he said, by the occasion to go out and hit a few balls himself.

It was difficult to get practice in the days before the match because we were the only members of our group in Dallas. We were fortunate that the local college players were keen to run for as long as we asked them, and they provided us with most of our opposition on the Sportface carpet which had been laid temporarily on the private court. The week passed in a jumble of interviews, receptions, practice sessions and interrupted meals, but at last the great day arrived.

My mind was brought back to the present as I heard the umpire call, *'Players ready? . . . Linesmen ready? . . . PLAY!'*

There was a hiss as Laver's first serve skidded through off the carpet. I missed the return. Another whistled by.

'Thirty love'

Suddenly an unexpected intrusion, a foot-fault was called. Rod glanced round enquiringly at the base-linesman who was doubling as foot-fault judge and pointed to his left foot with his racket. The linesman shook his head and explained that it was his right foot which had been touching the line. Outwardly Rod seemed composed. A beautiful bounce smash and the score was at 40-15. Again the linesman's voice – *'foot-fault!'*, and another questioning glance from Rod. It was the right foot again. Another good serve at 40-30 and Rod had got the start he wanted.

As we changed ends I could see that Rod was preoccupied. It was unusual to say the least that he should have been foot-faulted. I could not remember the last time I had seen it happen to him and this was hardly what he would have wanted. I held my serve to 30 for one-all and concentrated hard as Rod prepared to serve again.

We were both hitting the lines already and Rod leaped across to crunch a heavy backhand volley across the court for 30-all. We went to deuce and I found a cross-court backhand passing shot from the depths of my memory to give me the break point. Rod missed his first serve again. He looked more tense now – doubtless still worrying about those foot-faults. The rally began and suddenly there was the ball on my forehand as it leapt off the top of the net towards me. I drove it firmly across the court and it was past him. First blood to me.

I held for three-one by playing some short-angled volleys rather than the deep ones I usually employed against Rod. We both held until I was leading 5-4. I went to 40-30 – a set point that meant so much because a good start is all important in a match as big as this one was. My forehand volley missed the corner by a whisker.

'Deuce'

Then *'Advantage Rosewall'*

My second set point, and as Rod slipped in setting off to chase my cross-court backhand volley, I was home 6-4.

It had been a desperately close set and I knew that before long Rod would throw off the shackles of uncertainty that had held his game in check. He was still serving badly by his own standards and did not seem to be timing the ball properly on his returns.

The second set opened quietly.

When the ball flew off the racket frame into my eye at a critical moment in the third set Rod leapt the net and was the first to offer assistance. Fortunately no damage was done – but, as Rod said afterwards "I guess I hit him in the wrong eye!"

'One game all – second set'

Then in the third game I held three break points to take his serve but was thwarted each time by an ominously improving Laver.

'Laver leads by two games to one – second set'

Then, as I feared it might, the dam broke and Rod unleashed a series of unplayable shots to snatch my service for 3-1. Warming to his task, he held his own to love and broke me again after one deuce for 5-1. He then measured the distance for his service game.

'Fifteen-thirty'

Then there it was again – *'Foot-fault!'*. By now Rod must have come to terms with the problem and, hardly glancing at the linesman, he levelled at 30-all and two points later forced me to miss with a short forehand to draw level 6-1. After 69 minutes we were back where we had started.

My great chance came in the middle of the third set. I was seeing the ball really well now and broke Rod to 15 in the second game with a forehand return of serve to his feet off a really good first service. Then to 3-0 and 3-1 as Rod aced me. At last I'm going to stay ahead of him, I thought. But I had reckoned without Rod's genius. Just as I appeared to be getting on top he hit four clean winners on my service to cancel my advantage. It was 3-3 in no time. The seventh game was the turning point of the whole match. Five times Rod held a point to break my serve but on two of them he hit his forehand returns on the top of the frame and skied them into the roof. He did this on several occasions from the far end, perhaps because I was finding an uneven spot on the court which we had both noticed in practice. After flirting with death I finally went ahead 4-3 instead of facing a deficit.

So to 6-5 as we both held serve and Rod attempted to level again.

'Double fault, love fifteen'

Rod came racing in, punched a volley to my forehand and let my fore-hand cross-court passing shot go, only to see it fall on the line.

'Love thirty'

The advantage was short-lived. An ace from Rod after a let had been called.

'Thirty all'

Here I was, only two points from the set. I crouched low.

'Fault'

The second serve came at me like a bullet and skidded off the carpet as I swung my racket towards it. Suddenly there was a blinding light in my left eye as the ball flew off the frame into my face. I dropped the racket and clutched at my eye. Surely the match would not end like this. Rod leaped the net and ran towards me to see how serious the injury was. After two minutes I could see well enough to continue, though for the rest of the match the eye continued to water a lot. Back at the other end Rod buttoned down his mind again and had soon forced the tie-break at six all.

I held the first point and snatched Rod's first service point. Winning my next two took me to 4-1. Rod held another, 4-2, and I won again, 5-2. Now I only had to hold my next two service points for the set. As I came in behind my serve Rod followed in his return and guessed right to thump a volley towards my forehand side. I moved the right way more by instinct than anything else and punched my forehand volley past him. Pandemonium from the stands. At last I had reached set point but my next service point disappeared as I hesitated, waiting for the call of 'let' that did not come. As Rod served at 3-5 I knew I had to win quickly and when he missed with a volley I heaved a sigh of relief. We had been at it for two hours and three minutes and I was ahead by two sets to one.

As the fourth set began, I had a nagging feeling at the back of my mind that at any moment Rod would move into a higher gear and produce some of his unplayable tennis. I had seen him do this so often before and was thankful that only in that patch in the second set had he produced such tennis in this match. I had been trying to vary the length of my volleys. When you punch deep volleys at him – even good ones – he has the facility for making great running shots, the direction of which is disguised. He is sometimes not quite as quick to move forwards and the short volleys on the Sportface carpet were keeping low and skidding wide.

The first three games of the fourth set were too good to be true. Rod served two costly double faults – one in the first game, the other in the third – so that I was again leading 3-love, just as I had been in the third set. As I went to 40-30 in the fourth game I knew the match was as good as over if I could just hold on a few moments more. But Rod pulled me back to deuce. I ran for what seemed miles on the next point as we had a tremendous rally which ended with me wrong-footing Rod to get another point for 4-love. But again Rod denied me as he lunged for two vital volleys to bring back deuce.

Then, suddenly, it began. Two vicious topped returns and he had recovered one break of service. Growing in confidence with every second, Rod held comfortably for 2-3. Somehow I salvaged the sixth game to go 4-2 ahead but Rod swept through the seventh to love for 3-4. I had an agonising game on my service after that and, after another tremendous rally, I found a perfect short cross-court backhand volley that took me to 5-3.

No sign of nerves from Rod as he served to save the match. In no time it was 4-5 and I changed ends to deliver the *coup de grace.* While I was towelling down with the blue towel that matched my clothing, just as Rod's yellow towels matched his (no detail of organisation had been overlooked) I thought about those occasions when I had been in a similar position against Rod. Sometimes I had won but often he had escaped as he did in the 1965 Wembley final when I led by 5-3 in the final set only to lose it 6-8.

This time I would not let him off the hook. I came in behind my first serve to his backhand and was lucky to get my racket on his vicious topspin return. A second backhand flashed past me down the line.

'Love fifteen'

I tried a fast serve down the centre line and it beat him. There followed the moment I had dreaded – Rod connected with three perfect and unplayable backhands that I could only wonder at. The first was a cross-court passing shot that I did not even touch, the second went down the line and knocked the racket out of my hand as I dived for it, and the final one went clean as a whistle past me down the line. He had done it again. We were back on level terms at five-all and Rod was expanding almost visibly with confidence. How he does it I shall never know, but I have seen it happen so often now that I almost come to expect it.

I actually held a point to break Rod's next service game, but he finally went to 6-5 and I managed to play a good service game for 6-6. So here we were facing the tie-break yet again – the outcome of which would either take the match to a tense fifth set or give me victory.

Which side would he serve? To my backhand, I thought, and got set for the shot. As it came to my left I met it cleanly and projected a clean winner across him as he came in. A good start. Two points held by each of us and I was 3-2 ahead. Then 4-2 to me and 4-3 as Rod found yet another flashing backhand down the line. As he charged in on the next point trying to level matters I hoisted a high lob. He side-skipped backwards and let it bounce and as it fell he unleashed a huge smash. Perhaps due to the bright overhead lights he mis-hit it and the ball sailed over my base-line. As always with Rod there had been no compromise, but for once he had missed a shot at the vital moment. A deep forehand volley and I was serving at 5-4 – just two points from victory once again. A good volley and I was for the first time at match point. I made sure of getting in my first serve, a good deep one to his back-hand, and he went for his winner down the line – the shot that had broken me at 5-4. But this time, mercifully, it fell six inches wide and suddenly it was all over.

The scenes that followed will stay with me all my life – Neil Armstrong's words as he handed me the trophy; Mike Davies' joking reminder that the tax-man would see more of my cheque than I would; and my own

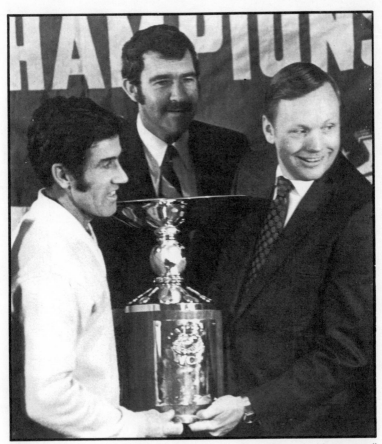

A giant step forward for tennis as Neil Armstrong hands me the trophy I knew so well, watched by Mike Davies of WCT. This victory was the culmination of all our dreams for professional tennis.

opportunity to thank everybody over the public address system. Rod, the true professional, managed to put a brave face on it, joking, 'I guess I hit him in the wrong eye!' It was perhaps ironic that Rod, who had beaten me so often in events all over the world, should have failed to produce his best form in the biggest match we had ever played against one another.

In the interviews that followed I know we both expressed our sincere feelings when we said how wonderful it felt to be part of a successful and growing game. I suppose I must count myself lucky that I have been given the chance to continue for so long at the highest level. I realise, of course, that the day must come when Father Time will have the final say, but until he issues his command, I shall do my best to put back something into the game in gratitude for all the pleasure it has given me, by appearing as often as my family commitments will allow and helping the development of the next generation of players through my association with the BP International Tennis Fellowship.

So ended a memorable year. If anyone had told me before it began that, during the course of it, I would be honoured by the Queen and the All England Club and that I would end it by being World Champion with my earnings falling only $2000 short of my record of the previous year, I would probably have said they were mad.

But I suppose, if I had really thought about it, I would have realised that almost any human goal is attainable if the will is there and the mind is directed aright, for tennis matches are played more in the mind than many people realise.

11. FIT TO PLAY

Winning that first WCT final in 1971 had made great demands upon my mental and physical reserves, and I was grateful for a period of rest at home. Although there are many new talented young players appearing on the scene, too few of them realise that to fulfil their potential they will need to train their bodies as well as practise their shots.

The advent of open tennis in 1968 brought a welcome honesty in the field of payments to players but inevitably meant that the competition for an ever-growing list of prize money events is getting tougher every year. This is as it should be.

It follows that only the fittest will survive and young players with aspirations to world class will need more than ever to build reserves of speed, strength and stamina during their developing years, just as I did when travelling with the Australian teams overseas between 1952 and 1957. The runs, exercises and endless sessions of 'threes' practice – two against one – were supervised by our Manager, Harry Hopman, who was never exactly popular with the players but knew very well how to get us fit and keep us that way! The intense periods of physical activity during our four-week build-up to Davis Cup Challenge Rounds in those years also got us into the peak of physical condition so that whatever our shortcomings as players we were never likely to fail on that score.

The strict self-discipline imposed by a routine of rigorous training serves to strengthen the mind as much as the body. Self-knowledge about one's hidden reserves of will power and energy is valuable at five-all in the fifth set. It comes from the ability to drive oneself hard in practice and training sessions.

The best training of all for tennis is the form of practice we have used in Australia for as long as I can remember – the 'threes' practice already referred to. Two players take up the volleying positions and fire a succession of balls at the player hitting groundstrokes who tries never to let the ball bounce twice and chases everything. The pressure on the lone player can be made intense by intelligent placing of the ball by the volleyers who fire a new ball to start a new rally as soon as the existing one breaks down. Even a short spell of this sort of work will tire and test the fittest of players. The value lies in the fact that the player must maintain the timing, rhythm and balance of each shot with aching muscles that are crying out for rest. This is where will-power is developed.

When it is apparent that the lone player is nearing breakdown point on his groundshots the roles are reversed with the two players moving back to the baseline and the lone player moving to the volleying position. He now has to volley every ball fired at him, trying to put away any easy ones for winners, and must attempt a smash at every lob he is given. If, reluctantly, the lob cannot be smashed then he should chase it, hit the return deep and move back towards the net for the next volley.

The great value of 'threes' lies in the fact that it can be used at all levels of the game by intelligent 'feeders' who exert the exact amount of pressure required – and no more. Unintelligent play by the two feeders could do more harm than good by destroying the technique and confidence of a player who is asked to work at too fast a pace for his stage of development. He must be stretched without being broken. Played properly this form of combined practice and training is tremendous fun and extremely satisfying – afterwards! It is valueless unless all three players are totally committed to giving everything they have got and are prepared to try for every ball. The whole tempo and atmosphere depend upon the enthusiasm and involvement of the players. I know that as I get older I need more of this sort of practice than ever to keep up my speed. Also I need to train more even though I probably do not do as much fitness training as I should.

A whole book could be written on general training methods designed to meet the requirements of tennis players. Suffice it to say that a basic level of general fitness is essential to any player wishing to compete seriously in tournaments. The quickest and safest way to achieve this sort of fitness is by some form of circuit training where you work against your own past performances. For those interested there are many books on this subject.

Running is basic to all forms of fitness and you will find that during periods of rest from competition you will need to maintain your level of stamina with brisk trots of between one and three miles two or three times a week. During the competition season, and assuming you are getting adequate time for on-court practice, a series of short, sharp sprints are best to maintain your speed. These bursts of about 15 yards, with jogs in between, repeat the sort of actions that you carry out in a match. An easy way to judge the distances is to sprint down the side of the court between the two baselines and jog very slowly along the stop netting at each end.

Skipping is another basic exercise which will benefit any player. Done properly it strengthens the arms as well as the legs and produces the lightness of movement that all players seek. Use as heavy a rope as you can find and vary the steps, some on both feet, some on one foot, some

During this week-long BP clinic in Sydney, one of the things I impressed upon these Australian youngsters was the need to develop themselves physically as well as to perfect their techniques.

with a skip between each turn of the rope, some without a skip and even some with two turns of the rope between each skip. Once you can skip like this non-stop for ten minutes you are in good condition.

All players need to have strong wrists so any wrist strengthening exercises are worth doing. Squeezing a squash ball in the pocket is an unobtrusive way of improving strength and, at home, it is a good idea to use a wrist-roller, easly made from a broom handle or an old racket handle sawn off above the grip. Get a suitable piece of wood about 9 in. long and bore a hole in the centre. Through the hole attach a piece of strong cord about 3–4 ft. long and attach a weight to it – a brick will do. Wind the weight up and down by using the wrists to twist the stick and keep the forearms parallel to the ground and the elbows in to the sides.

Strong tummy muscles too, are essential for any serious player. There are many exercises which will add strength but the easiest ones to perform are sit-ups. Lie flat on your back, clasp your hands behind your head and sit up, pushing your forehead towards your knees and keeping your legs straight.

Young players who are physically deficient in any areas of their bodies should seek the advice of an expert – preferably a coach who is experienced in modern training methods. Methods of increasing strength, like isometrics and weight training, can be very valuable in certain cases and under proper supervision. However, ignorant use of these methods can be harmful so take care to get good advice. A tennis player needs adequate strength but not excess strength – and certainly not strength at the expense of suppleness. Flexible joints and supple movements are vital to success and they could be hindered by using unintelligent forms of training.

My remarks thus far have been confined to serious and ambitious players but they apply, in lesser degree, equally to the keen amateur. It has been my experience in life that people get the most fun out of their chosen hobby or sport when they work at it to the limit of the time and opportunity available. The important thing is to practise intelligently. If you cannot find an opponent try to find a wall where there is space enough for you to hit your ground-strokes, volleys, serves and even smashes against it. Most of the leading players know the value of wall practice in re-grooving shots that have become troublesome. Concentration and footwork are improved too on the wall – the rallies can never be won and the wall is tireless.

Above all devote your full attention to whatever practice or training you are doing at all times. If I were asked to name one aspect of tennis that is the biggest weakness of players of all levels I would probably say concentration. However good your shots, however fast your movement and reflexes, all is lost if the mind is not controlling every move. Concentration is something which needs to be practised just like your backhand and it is done by shutting out everything from your mind except the job in hand. This sounds easy and for some lucky ones it is but for most of us concentration requires constant polishing by industrious and intelligent practice.

12. RETURN TO DALLAS

Little did I think, when I won that first WCT final in November 1971, that six short months later Rod Laver and I would be back in Dallas shooting it out again for a first prize of $50,000. Nor did I imagine that we were about to contest a match that many who saw described later as the best of the countless battles we have had over the years.

And if I had known beforehand of the degree of physical and mental pain I was to suffer, perhaps I might not even have begun. I do know that if I had not spent long years training and practising in the way I have just described, then I would never have survived.

It all began with the last ten tournaments of the newly-arranged year adapted to suit American TV which ended in May instead of November and so counted the second half of the 1971 year twice. Accordingly, it was no surprise that the same eight players who had assembled in Houston in November 1971 should have won through to the '72 play-offs in Dallas, but the draw was different. Our quarter-final line-up this time was Rod Laver against John Newcombe and Cliff Drysdale against Marty Riessen in the top half with Arthur Ashe against Tom Okker and Bob Lutz against me in the bottom half.

In 1971 we had played in Houston for the quarter-final and semi-final matches and had transferred to the Memorial Auditorium, Dallas, for the final. This year, in response to the wonderful support that the Dallas public had given us the previous November, all the matches were played in the Southern Methodist University arena there which I knew well from tour visits with the pros in the old days.

As first and second seeds Rod and I played our quarter-final matches first, on the Wednesday, so that we had a day's rest before our semi-finals on Friday. This raised some controversy among the players who felt it was unfair that a player whose quarter-final was played on the Thursday would have no rest. This is something which WCT might want to consider in the future.

As defending champion I played the opening match and, as I had not played Bob very often, I was slightly apprehensive about the outcome. My form in the last two weeks had been patchy to say the least. I had beaten the New Zealand youngster Brian Fairlie twice in the opening rounds but then had lost to Emerson in the mile-high altitude of Denver and Newcombe had beaten me in Las Vegas. This victory gave John just enough points to qualify for Dallas.

My form during 1972 had been fair – for an old man – and I had either won the tournament or had lost to the eventual winner (except for the loss to Emerson in Denver) so I was quietly confident. My concentration against Bob Lutz was not too good to begin with, but I eventually took hold of it to beat him in five hard sets which gave me the sort of tough introduction that I needed to bring me to form.

Rod was altogether too severe for John Newcombe and the next night Ashe got past Okker without major problems. Riessen produced the drama by climbing back from an apparently hopeless situation to win an excellent but exhausting match against Drysdale.

My semi-final with Ashe went very much the way I had hoped. With Arthur it all depends on how he is serving and that day I was able to get enough low returns back to prevent him from thumping those winners that he loves off high returns. My winning margin was 6-4 6-2 7-6 so I was able to relax in a happy frame of mind on Saturday.

Rod started badly against Riessen, losing the opening two sets 6-4 6-4. However, he surged back to lose only three games more as he swept a tiring Riessen from the court 6-1 6-2 6-0. One could sympathise with Riessen for having to play two tough matches on consecutive days.

So to the showdown – the second major confrontation in six months between Rod and me. As in the previous year statistics pointed to a Laver win. In our previous two matches Rod had two wins against me and as Tony Trabert, our referee spun the racket, I wondered if the memory of last year's dramatic match was in the back of Rod's mind. Certainly I was thinking about it and trying to get into the right frame of mind.

Rod and I have played so often against one another over the past ten years that it would have been easy to be discouraged because of his high percentage of wins but each time I try to tell myself that this is a fresh start, a match that would be won on the merits of the shots played and not influenced by Rod's considerable lead in our personal series. Many times we have fought out close and exciting battles but, as it transpired, none of them had been quite as dramatic or tense as the one we were about to start. It became clear afterwards that by altering two or three vital points the outcome of the match could have been altered. With today's tie-break this element of chance has been thrown into the arena to add to a player's problems and it is all the more important to make the lucky breaks tell for you.

Some of our close points turned on service deliveries. In the course of the match I managed to find one ace somewhere in the first set, in the fifth game, which was the first game I won. Rod served a vital ace in the fifth set when I was standing at match point when he served at 4-5. The double faults played a more important role. It was Rod's serving rather than mine that was the dominant feature. He was either very good or rather weak and the total of double faults he served – ten in all to my four – reflected the difference between us there. One in particular was costly for Rod when he was serving at three points to two in the tie-break of the final set. In fact this was tragic for him and must have given me the chance to stay alive.

The match began in a flurry of Laver brilliance. In no time at all I was 4-0 behind although I did not feel that I was playing badly! Rod was simply going for his shots and making them. I was desperately hoping to find some rhythm and confidence so when I held my serve for 1-4 I heaved a sigh of relief. I had a point in the next game for 2-4 but was denied it and Rod moved on to 5-1. After holding my own delivery for 2-5 I managed to get through him at last and with a break and another service game I crept up to 4-5. I felt Rod was wavering slightly as I held several points for 5-5 but he was not in the mood to be denied and, when he climbed up on my short lob to ram home his smash giving him the opening set 6-4, I knew that I had a battle on my hands.

The statistics of overheads played in that opening set were interesting. Rod hit three winning smashes and made one error; my score was three winners to no errors. It was a similar pattern through the other sets, so that at the finish Rod had made 15 winning overheads to my 17 but his errors totalled six to my one (which I seem to remember happened in the third set). These figures emphasise the importance of the lob – a shot you have to use constantly against Rod to keep him back from his favourite launching pad in the forecourt.

As we began the second set I was expecting Rod's confidence to surge as a result of winning the opener. It did not help matters when I opened the set with a double fault, but after surviving a 30-40 situation, I saved the point with a cross court backhand volley and finally held my serve. After four break points I was 2-0 ahead and to my amazement I won the set 6-0. As that final shot of the set landed in – a well placed backhand down the line out of his reach – I tried to remember the last time I had won a 6-0 set against him. I couldn't think of a single occasion. It was a strange experience, especially when I had expected the opposite to happen.

This, not surprisingly, was the shortest of our sets – 54 points in all, and already the TV commentators were saying that I was looking tired. To open the third set I succeeded at last with a wide serve to his backhand, a shot I had been trying to find all evening, but he whacked a clean winner down the line. Somehow I held, and games went with serve until

Rod was serving at 2-3. After some exciting play I got to game point but put up another short lob. I did finally break through for 4-2, held for 5-2 with a good angled overhead but could not prevent Rod from drawing up to 3-5. Then without much trouble I got home 6-3 to lead by two sets to one.

During that set Rod's serve had been erratic and I noticed he changed rackets at the start of the fourth. I had been making some good returns which had kept the pressure on him and Rod had suffered perhaps more than me from a few doubtful calls – not that there were many considering the difficulty of sighting the ball on the fast Sportface carpet. At least this time Rod had not been foot-faulted – a factor which had robbed him of rhythm and confidence the previous November.

The fourth set presented me with a golden opportunity to force a quick victory. I found a cross court backhand winner to break Rod to go 2-1 ahead and held for 3-1. I had played Rod often enough to know that in this situation he is at his most dangerous and told myself that it would not happen to me this time as it had so often in the past. But suddenly in the sixth game there I was – 0-40 behind from three incredible Laver winners and he had done it again. From 3-3, Rod went ahead on serve to 4-3 and it seemed almost inevitable that the tie-break would be necessary to separate us.

I got a dream start in the tie-break, led 2-0 and had a backhand volley for 3-0 – but missed it. Then it was all Rod. He won six of the next seven points with flailing winners and here we were at two sets all. In the course of the set we had played 68 points. I had won 32 and lost 36 – a difference of merely four points which was exactly the margin of the tie-break, 7-3 to Rod.

We had been playing for two and a half hours and it was really no surprise that we were heading for yet another deciding set. The colour television equipment needed a lot of light and it was really hot. Earlier I remember that my shirt was wet through, but by now I had become so dehydrated from the heat and all the running that my shirt had dried on my back. Also I was getting very tired. As I got my mind down to the job of somehow winning this deciding set, my legs felt as though they had been filled with lead, but oddly, the pain was bearable during the rallies.

When Rod and I play well against one another we play a mixture of all types of tennis. Despite the fast surface, at the start of that fifth set we had several excellent baseline rallies, because we were both keeping such a good length. I held for 1-0 with a good backhand volley and thought it ironic that the 3-0 lead in the tie-break had escaped me when I had missed the same shot just a few moments earlier.

As Rod obliged with two missed backhand volleys I broke for 2-0. The excitement caused a spectator to shout from somewhere up in the stands and we had to ask Mike Blanchard, the umpire, to quieten him. I held for 3-0 and began to wonder if we were going to repeat the second set. Rod steadied himself to serve – it was a big game for both of us. He missed two forehands for 0-30 but then I hit two lobs that were too short – 30-30. At deuce Rod played some great shots to hold a game point, but his eighth double fault of the match brought back deuce. Then I found a perfect lob on to the line for an advantage and a point for 4-0. Yet on my next return I hit the wildest forehand of 1972. Ultimately, Rod held his serve, the seventh game point of this seesaw game and I had had four chances to break.

The next game, too, was desperately close and after five deuces I went ahead 4-1. Through my mind there flashed the memory of last year's final when I had had Rod in a similar situation only to see him raise his game to level matters. I wondered how I could avert it this time. The inevitable happened in the seventh game as I served for my 5-2 lead. I slipped behind 0-40, recovered to 30-40 but hit the net with my approach shot. We were nearing the three and a half hour mark now and you could actually feel the tension in the air as we battled against fatigue and each other.

Ominously Rod served a love game for 4-4. I held for 5-4, desperately hoping to break Rod's serve to avoid the tie-break. Somehow I forced myself to match point at 30-40 with some good returns but Rod found that ace down the centre line that I mentioned earlier, to deny me. In no time it was 5-5.

Now, quite suddenly I felt exhausted. I tried not to think about the fourth set when I had had the break or my break in this fifth set – let alone that possible 4-0 lead that had been denied me.

I had been returning softly, concentrating on getting the ball to Rod's feet just as Pancho Gonzales did some years ago at Wembley when he surprisingly beat Rod in the BBC2 tournament. Perhaps, I thought, it was not time to go for my returns, so on Rod's next service game at 5-6 I did play some firmer ones. It nearly paid dividends for I was within reach of him but failed to follow in a good lob at 40-30 and was forced to lob again only to see him hit his winning smash.

Inevitably, I suppose, here we were in the tie-break of the final set – right down to our last reserves of energy. I served first and held my point with a backhand volley. At 1-1 Rod served wide to my forehand – I could not return it and he went to 2-1. He hit my next serve off his backhand for a clean winner, 3-1 to him. I won my next point and then Rod served at 3-2 – a double fault to make it 3-3 – what a moment to falter! I hit up what felt like a good lob but it was called long, so it was 3-4 and my serve.

My forehand volley slid out over the sideline, for 3-5 and I still had one more point to serve. I held it but now Rod was 5-4 with two service points to win for the match.

I thought he might go for my backhand so I decided to step in and hit it early across court. Fortunately I was right and my return went like a bullet and I watched his forehand half-volley balloon over the baseline. Five all. This time, I thought, he must try his favourite centre serve. Sure enough, down it came and I drove a backhand down the line past him. So here I was with my second match point at 6-5 and my own serve to come. I decided to get the first one in deep, but it was a let. Again I went for depth and, with the utmost relief, saw Rod net his backhand return. At last, after three and three-quarter hours it was all over.

The crowd of spectators who had been growing more and more excited as the match built to its climax erupted around the stadium and there was pandemonium as we collected ourselves at the net.

At the presentation ceremony, Michael Davies, the Executive Director of WCT, summed it up for most of them, 'That is probably the greatest tennis match that I have ever seen in my life. There should have been two winners out there today – in fact tennis and the public really came out the winners.'

I could hardly find any words myself and I almost dropped the Cup as it was handed to me. More than the first prize of $50,000, more than the new car which went with the title, more than the title itself, I was thrilled that when it really came to it I had, at the age of 37, still been able to find the sort of inspiration that I feared might have left me for ever. Rod could not have been more gracious or sporting in defeat and to him I give the last word. 'Well, I always say third time lucky – so everyone had better look out next year.'

Sadly for Rod, we now know that Stan Smith became the third World Champion of Tennis when he beat Arthur Ashe in a thrilling 1973 final. Then it was the turn of John Newcombe, who was pressed to the limit by the teenage Swedish sensation Bjorn Borg in a wonderful finish to the 1974 competition.

Perhaps 1975 will at last be Laver's year, for the World Championship of Tennis is the only major title missing from his overloaded trophy cupboard. It would be a most fitting finale to his fabulous career if he were to succeed.

13. FRIENDS AND RIVALS

During the course of my 25 years in tennis I have been competing against some of the finest players the game has ever seen – men like Frank Sedgman, Jack Kramer, Pancho Gonzales, and Lew Hoad. How they would compare with the great champions of the past, like America's Bill 'Mr Tennis' Tilden; the French Musketeers, Henri Cochet, Rene Lacoste, and Jean Borotra; Britain's extrovert hero, Fred Perry; or the quiet American, Don Budge, I can only guess. Suffice to say that the champion of any era is only as good as he has to be so that if any of these past great players were living in the tougher competitive situation that exists today, they would probably still excel.

Some years ago I compiled a ranking list of the ten best players I had competed against when they were all at their peaks. Rod Laver was in the top position – and he probably still would be if I sat down to do this list again now. However, it is a measure of the fast changing pattern of the modern pressure game that Ilie Nastase and Stan Smith were jointly last then, and Jimmy Connors did not appear on the list at all. This time I have not attempted to compare the eras for space does not permit the inclusion of the present champions or the promising younger men like Bjorn Borg or 'Bill' Vilas who have hardly begun what should surely become outstanding careers. However, I have delved into my store-house of memories to parade some old friends and rivals before you.

JOHN BROMWICH

As a boy I remember once going to watch a match at the White City tennis club in Sydney – it was an early round of the New South Wales Championships. John Bromwich was playing a less well-known overseas player and as I approached the court I could see Brom's head falling forward on one shoulder as he dragged himself back towards the baseline, a picture of utter misery. I thought he must be in trouble – perhaps I was about to witness a sensational upset. Turning to a friend as I reached the courtside I asked the score and was told that Brom was leading 6-0 6-0, 3-1 and his misery came from the fact that he had just lost a game he thought he should have won. Brom was like that. It actually hurt him to lose a point but in the course of his career there weren't many that he lost needlessly. He was an unusual player using two hands on the right-hand side of his body and one hand on the left-hand side so that most people would have thought of him as a lefthander. But he served right-handed. He came to his best just as the second world war opened. After the war I am told that his shots carried less pace than they used to. Although I did not, as many people believed, pattern my game on his it used to thrill me to watch the delicacy of his touch and the refinement of his clever use of the angles of the court.

I saw him in 1948 shortly before he left for Europe where he was to reach the Wimbledon final only to lose tragically to the American Bob Falkenburg after holding match points.

He had no big shots but he bamboozled opponents with angled drives, low lobs and soft balls to the feet, shots that carried no pace but were always in an awkward place. He had a very soft serve and relied on accuracy and placement for effect. The racket he used was the lightest of any man player I have known weighing a little over $12\frac{1}{2}$ ounces with a tiny handle more like a pencil than a normal racket handle and strung extremely slack. Big hitting players used to try to attack his serve and come to the net, a tactic which Brom enjoyed facing for his passing shots were his forte. On the right side, his double-hander carried disguise and control and his touch with the left hand was equally good.

He will perhaps be remembered best as a doubles player, for he won doubles titles all over the world with different partners – Adrian Quist, Frank Sedgman, Colin Long, Billy Sidwell and even with me when I was raw, inexperienced, overawed at being paired with him and incredulous at the way we won the Tasmanian title together.

ROY EMERSON
There can have been no fitter man playing tennis than Roy Emerson. A complete athlete, dedicated to the ideal of super-fitness, Roy's constant aggression on the court won him two Wimbledon titles in 1964 and 65, two French Championships titles in 1963 and 67, two US titles in 1961 and 64 and no fewer than six Australian titles in 1961, 63, 64, 65, 66 and 67. Apart from Rod Laver, Roy is the only player in this list who has won all four of the major championships. And his doubles record is remarkable. With a variety of partners he has won 19 major doubles titles but none gave him more pleasure than his 1971 success at Wimbledon with Rod Laver which, amazingly, was Rod's first doubles title there. Roy once described himself as a high-class hacker. This over-modest view emphasises his willingness to chase and retrieve all day in the relentless search for points and games. At any rate his hacking utterly dominated the pre-open days of the mid '60s and his Davis Cup record

of 15 winning rubbers out of 18 when he was eight times in the winning team is a record. I suppose he is the outstanding example of what the Australian training methods can do to get the maximum out of a player's potential. Roy has been a 101 percenter all his life. He never knew he was beaten so one could never relax against him and his capacity for work was quite staggering. In addition he has remained one of the fairest and most likeable opponents I can ever remember meeting. Nowadays he spends more time organising and conducting the tennis programmes at

A typical scrambling recovery by Roy Emerson from deep behind the baseline made possible by his supreme fitness and unquenchable appetite for practice.

the ranch he operates with Laver. His enormous energy and natural good humour fit him well for the task of inspiring hard work in others and I am sure he will make a success of this latest business venture.

PANCHO GONZALES

My introduction to professional tennis occurred on the 14th January 1957. Before 13,000 people on the centre court at Kooyong where, as an amateur, I had played many thrilling matches, I faced the man who many regard as one of the greatest of all tennis players – the Mexican-American Pancho Gonzales. Shall I ever forget that baptism of fire as I stood there facing a barrage of lethal serves and brutal volleys that had me scampering to all corners of the stadium? I lost 9-7 in the fifth set and realised that in the weeks ahead as our tour in America got under way I would be in for some stirring battles.

Pancho Gonzales' record was cut short by his early decision to join the professional ranks to tour with Jack Kramer. In 1948 and 1949 when he was only 19 and 20 he had won the US Championships. He turned pro in 1950 and was at the top of the game, or near it, until 1972. What a span that is, 1948 to 1972. Yes, he actually won a tournament that year, one of the US indoor circuit tournaments in Des Moines where he beat the young French Davis Cup player George Goven in a five-set final. When one considers what might have been had he not turned professional so early in his career one realises that he could have amassed a record to surpass any before him and probably any yet to come. It makes one wish that Open tennis had come much earlier.

I suppose the Gonzales fire, which utterly consumes him on a court in the quest of winning the match he is involved in, is the driving force that keeps him going today. He is a tremendous competitor – intimidating, frightening, glorious, arrogant – the adjectives are endless, for he has been one of the game's immense characters.

His game has been built around one of the most fluent, easy service actions you could ever wish to see. It has given him a fast, well-disguised delivery that is a nightmare to return when he is playing with confidence. Most of his tennis, at least in his best playing years, was played on the indoor arenas of America where the canvas court with its fast bounce suited his game ideally. Behind this fearsome service he brought the qualities of concentration and agility to his volleying that made him almost impossible to pass or lob. In the forecourt he was like a cat ready to pounce whichever way you decided to hit the ball and if you chose to

The mighty service of Pancho Gonzales has daunted countless opponents, for the past 20 years. Here it helps him to win the Pinch Grand Masters title at Forest Hills in 1974 at the age of 46.

lob there he would be suddenly climbing an invisible ladder to thump down that enormous smash.

Although Gonzales did not play much of his tennis on slow clay-courts until Open tennis came along, he proved that he could win on them. In 1968, for example, he beat Roy Emerson twice in Paris and he had beaten even the great Pancho Segura on clay – which is saying a lot for any tennis player.

His ground strokes were shots of his own invention – sound but at the same time unorthodox, because he could use his wrist (particularly on the forehand) to disguise the direction of his drive until the last moment. It always seemed that he waited until you had committed yourself before he decided he would play his shot.

Above all Gonzales was a great competitor with a champion's pride in his performance that simply refused to admit defeat. He was a great mover so that court coverage was never a problem and a wonderful player of the second shot in a rally – always an important aspect of a champion's make-up. He was a master of timing, his effort to pounce on the chance once he had created it, and his amazingly quick reflexes, enabled him to pick up surprising shots to turn apparent defeat into victory.

The significant thing about Gonzales is that he always has created excitement wherever he has played and even today I believe that if you were to ask the tennis loving people who they most enjoyed watching many of them would still answer 'Pancho'. Happily there are still opportunities to watch the old tiger in competitive situations through the extraordinary development of the senior game in America. Watching him beat Torben Ulrich in the over-45 final at Forest Hills in 1974 I marvelled at the enduring skill and competitive fire that drove him to victory on the sort of sweltering afternoon on which most men of his age would have had a beer in hand and feet on the mantelpiece.

LEW HOAD

I first met Lew Hoad in 1946. The United States Davis Cup team consisting of Jack Kramer, Ted Schroeder, Gardnar Mulloy and Frank Parker had taken the Cup from the holders, Australia, with a 5-0 victory in Melbourne against Dinny Pails, John Bromwich and Adrian Quist. The American team came on to Rockdale, a small Sydney suburb where I lived, to play exhibition matches, and Lew and I had been invited to play the warm-up match which juniors were often asked to do in those days. We were both 12 years old and, naturally, it was a great thrill for us to appear on the same court as our great heroes.

Even then as I chased against the raking shots of the young giant across the net – for so he appeared to the eyes of another 12-year-old – I recognised in Lew a touch of greatness. Little did either of us realise how much our paths would cross in later years or how many wonderful tennis triumphs and disasters were in store.

Lew Hoad has a record to show that he was one of the game's truly great players. His game developed early and even at the age of 15 his great physical strength enabled him to play on level terms with the best men. He hit the ball hard and firmly without compromise and without fear. He had the priceless ability to hit a great shot at the right moment. Lew was blessed with a good temperament, too, and had another priceless ability – the knack of raising his game when the occasion demanded. His only lapse was in the Davis Cup challenge round of 1954 when he and I lost to those two great American competitors Vic Seixas and Tony Trabert. The year before Lew had been the architect of a sensational challenge round victory for us when he beat Tony Trabert 7-5 in the fifth set in one of the most emotional matches I can ever remember watching.

Lew's great year was 1956. He started well in Australia, where I was unlucky enough to meet him in the final in one of his devastating moods. He won Paris that year and Wimbledon, where again I was his victim. It was almost with sadness that I got my revenge at Forest Hills, for the victory robbed Lew of his Grand Slam and prevented him from winning his first US title.

It was after Lew turned Professional following his second Wimbledon victory in 1957 that we renewed our personal clashes and developed our friendship which lasts until this day. We travelled to many strange places together as the professional game developed in America and survived the difficult years to see the amazing explosion of Open tennis in 1968.

Lew's game inevitably varied a good deal. For a great player his only real weakness was the occasional lapse in his concentration. It was this that was responsible for the bad losses that to his many fans must have read like a misprint in the newspaper. I remember well back in 1949 when we were sometimes teamed in doubles together he would be looking at the match on the next court and got me doing the same thing. We can laugh about those days now, but at the time the loss of a string of quick games used to upset our advisers more than ourselves.

Lew was one of the most commanding hitters of a tennis ball I have ever faced. When he was really on his game he was almost frightening to play against. There was nothing he could not do and his strength of arm and wrist enabled him to create shots that you will not find in any of the text books. He would see the ball so early on service return – even against servers of Gonzales' and Sedgman's calibre that he would flick them disdainfully past the advancing server for clean winners. It is fortunate for those of us whose careers coincided with his that he was not always at a peak because the game would have been too one-sided for even his most ardent fans to enjoy. Had he been more consistent he might have had a record as good as Laver and then might have headed any list of all time greats.

Lew had everything – a wonderful physique, split-second timing, fast reflexes and amazing agility which, allied to his strength, enabled him to bound about the court or leap for a smash with cat-like agility. His forehand was always good and as he grew in confidence and experience his backhand became almost better. Until his back trouble began to spoil his game after 1958 he had a wonderful service. He had one serve in particular, a wide ball to the forehand, the like of which I have never faced from anyone else. Despite its apparent slice – and I can assure you it carried you right outside the court – it used to kick back into the body of the receiver. Even when you knew it was likely to come this serve was disconcerting and won him many valuable points.

I shall always be glad that my time in tennis coincided with Lew's as it enabled me to appreciate what a great person he is, as well as a fine exponent of the art of tennis. Generous, almost to a fault, Lew would help anyone in need. It is fitting that with his wife Jenny and their attractive children, he should have built a tennis ranch in Southern Spain where they both derive continuing happiness by again helping the ambitious youngsters of today. I am certain that many of them will carry away from Fuengirola more than just an improved forehand.

JACK KRAMER

I first met Mr Kramer, as I called him then, at the end of 1946 during the exhibition matches at Rockdale already referred to. I was just 12 so I had not travelled to Melbourne to watch the Challenge Round but I remember listening to it intently on the radio. The American win by five matches to nil impressed my young mind greatly so that when I knew the US team was coming to the Sydney suburb in which I lived, to play a series of exhibition matches for the Illawara Hard Courts Association I was determined not to miss them.

I remember being greatly impressed by Kramer's game, which was based on a big serve and heavy, well controlled ground shots. I remember thinking how solid his forehand and backhand seemed with the head of the racket flowing right through the ball. His service was as smooth as silk and he seemed to hit the second one just as hard as the first.

Jack Kramer, perhaps more than any single individual, has been responsible for the growth of the professional game as player, promoter, and now executive director of ATP. Here he is near the end of his playing career at one of the Wembley tournaments in the 1950s.

As I came to understand more about Jack Kramer in our matches together as professionals when he was past his best I learned how sound his technique really was so that he could play successfully on any surface. He had a great competitive streak – something the Americans call 'killer instinct' and a tremendous, deep concentration. His will to win was enormous and, towards the end of his career, even drove him to play when his injured back used to give him great pain.

I first played him the year I turned professional in 1957 but I remember reading of his victory against Frank Sedgman only four years earlier on their 100-match tour across the United States. We spent the year in South America, Europe and the United States and all the time Jack's machine-like game and excellent footwork, plus an uncanny knowledge of the right shot to play made him a fearsome opponent. Jack has always been one of the game's thinkers and as a promoter he knew what the public wanted and set about giving it to them. In those far off days of the divided worlds of tennis this meant signing up the leading amateurs of the year to play head to head tours against the reigning pro. champion.

It was natural, therefore, when Open tennis arrived in 1968 and the new breed of professionals started to organise themselves, that they should look to Jack for advice. It was logical, too, that they should ask him to become the first Executive Director of the Association of Tennis Professionals when it was formed in 1972. No one has a deeper knowledge or love of the game than Jack and it was sad that he became the centre of controversy for leading ATP to boycott Wimbledon in 1973 over the Pilic Affair. Fortunately he has lived that down and now serves on the Professional Tennis Council where he can still bring his unrivalled understanding of the game to bear in helping to solve its present problems.

ROD LAVER

I first got to know Rodney George Laver in 1956. He and Bob Mark had been attached to the Australian touring team of Mal Anderson, Ashley Cooper, Neale Fraser and myself under the captaincy of Cliff Sproule. The idea was that these two promising juniors should go on the trip for the experience. They certainly got plenty of that – Rod won the US Junior title at Kalamazoo that year – the beginning of an international trophy bag that is so vast by now that probably even he has forgotten most of the titles he has won around the world.

Where does one begin when trying to assess a man with such a formidable record. Although it is difficult, if not impossible, to compare the eras, Rod Laver must certainly be high up on the list of all-time great players. Nobody before or since has ever won the Grand Slam twice as Rod did in 1962 and 1969 – the second time in the new era of Open tennis, which was a much greater test than anyone had faced before.

I have always admired Rod for the way he pulled his weight in the tough days we went through in the professional game between 1963 and 1965. Rod really put himself behind pro. tennis and was always a great friend of all the players. He is a wonderful example to the young players today, some of whom forget just how hard he worked in the struggle to reach the top.

Rod's game improved a great deal when he turned professional in 1962. Until then only his close friend and doubles partner, Roy Emerson, was able to give him any real opposition. His decision to join the pro. ranks enabled us to keep the game going and, in fact, though the struggle has been hard we have never looked back from that moment.

Rod has a tremendous attitude to competition with a will to win the equal of any great champion. As an opponent he is feared and respected and all of us look to see if he is in the other half of the draw before we notice who we play ourselves. Like a true champion he has always done the right thing on and off the court.

When he is playing confidently I cannot think of a more destructive tennis machine than Rod Laver. He is one of the toughest players you could ever have the misfortune to meet. He hits the ball hard, moves like lightning and has no weaknesses – so how do you beat him? To be honest you do not, unless a chink appears in his armour. It used to be his forehand volley but that's no weakness now. Occasionally it is his service which still lets him down at times. However, in the last five or six years his service has improved out of sight. He is hitting even harder now than he used to and the wicked spin that he can command and the disguise he can achieve – particularly when running flat out to make his shot, makes him a really hazardous opponent to face.

And apart from the tennis in all the years we have travelled together and in all the matches and tournaments we have competed, Rod has always been there ready to attend the press conferences, the TV spots, the store appearances, anything that was needed to put the show on the road. He and I had a most nostalgic return to Davis Cup tennis after more than a decade's absence when we won the great trophy back from the United States in 1973.

Rod has been a tremendous asset to the game; he has won more than a million dollars from tennis and has truly earned it. He is a great sportsman, the greatest of players and a great ambassador for tennis. His future? Like most players he has had his share of injuries but he seems to be completely fit again now. His recent match with Jimmy Connors in Las Vegas showed that in brief spells he can be devastating but, like me, he has decided to restrict his tournament appearances from now on. I have no doubt that he will continue to win matches but, I suspect, that like me too he will derive just as much pleasure and satisfaction from his coaching activities at the camps he conducts with his old friend Roy Emerson.

ADRIAN QUIST

Adrian was a little older than John Bromwich and lost his best years to the war. In fact he retired from active championship play soon after the game was resumed following the war. He was a serve and volley man and loved nothing better than the fierce volleying exchanges of a fast men's doubles. He was a perfect partner for John Bromwich, the man with quick reflexes and fast darting movements at the net who could cut off spectacularly those short balls in the forecourt engineered by Bromwich's cunning.

I first saw Adrian at the New South Wales Championships in 1945 and remember marvelling at his bustling energy that took him always forwards for the volley. Perhaps I was also impressed by the fact that Adrian, like me, was only 5 ft 7 in. in height. He was a natural hero for me at that age. His groundstrokes were adequate but there was a weakness on the backhand side that could be exposed in singles. However, in the second court in a doubles match it was well nigh impossible to find that backhand. He stood over well beyond the sideline to receive the serve inviting a fast one down the centre. Many players tried to serve high-kickers to his backhand but he knew how to move in early and clip the return short to the feet of the incoming server and be right on top of the net to ram the volley home for a winner. His biggest singles win was probably his 1939 Challenge Round success against Bobby Riggs who was then the reigning Wimbledon Champion.

With Bromwich he won the Australian doubles title for eight years between 1938 and 1959 – and had already won it twice before that with Turnbull.

The whole tennis world was thrilled when he decided to make the trip to Wimbledon with Bromwich in 1950 where they fittingly won the doubles title in five sets against two Australian rivals Geoff Brown and Billy Sidwell.

FRANK SEDGMAN

I suppose the man who had the greatest influence on me as a young player was Frank Sedgman who, in the early fifties, was one of the outstanding players in the world. I was only 16 when I first played him. It was 1951 and we met in the semi-final of the Queensland Championships.

For me it was a tremendous thrill actually to be pitting my wits against a man who had won titles all over the place. I lost in five sets, but the next week in the semi-final of the New South Wales Championships in Sydney, Frank obviously moved into a higher gear to beat me in straight sets.

At the end of that year it appeared that he would turn professional for Jack Kramer who, at that time, was running the pro. group in America. However, a well-timed wedding gift to his wife avoided that and he remained with the Australian Davis Cup team to win the Cup at the end of 1952 with the help of Ken McGregor and Mervyn Rose. Then, however, he did sign for Kramer.

I got to know Frank much better when I turned professional in 1957 and I found him to be a great companion and a tremendous sportsman and competitor.

He was just about the fastest volleyer I have ever seen on a tennis court and it was this dazzling speed and uncanny anticipation which made him so difficult to play against. He was powerful but lithe physically and hit the ball early and firmly without ever having the weight of·shot that Lew Hoad possessed. He was solid on both forehand and backhand drives and he loved to run around short second serves to smite a forehand return and rush into the net to harrass his opponent. The bluff worked often and it taught me how important it is to take the offensive on a tennis court at every opportunity.

Frank had a good first serve without it ever being a complete cannonball and his only weakness really was a tendency to serve occasional short second services. This offered his opponents a chance to take the initiative in the rallies before he did – a rare thing in matches he played.

With Frank it was constant attack; he could volley from anywhere on his side of the net and could control the ball so well that he could get to the net from a volley he had hit near his own baseline. I suppose his forehand volley was his really outstanding shot and it must be classed on the same level for quality as Budge Patty's famous forehand volley.

I always think of Sedgman as the first player to demonstrate the value of constant all-out attack. He could turn defence into attack because of his extremely fast reflexes and the volleying ability that I have already referred to. It was not the same sort of all-out attack that we see now. He was more orthodox in that his returns were firm blocks or drives taken early, and not the vicious whipped drives which the top players today seem to be turning to in the search for even greater pace and attacking power against the server.

Frank Sedgman had a wonderful record in Davis Cup play for Australia. In 1951 he beat both Vic Seixas and Ted Schroeder, and the following year he beat Seixas again and Tony Trabert. At Wimbledon the same year, 1952, he won the title that seemed as if it would elude him when he beat Jaroslav Drobny in a four-set final.

As a professional he played many memorable matches – none more so than his whirlwind 1953 victory against the reigning world champion, Pancho Gonzales at Wembley, London. Equally exciting and memorable was a match he lost to Gonzales at Wembley – that thrilling five-set final in 1956 which held the crowds spellbound until 12.40 am and is still talked of as one of the game's classics. It is marvellous that the development of the Grand Masters tour – that group of past champions over the age of 45 – is enabling the present generation to catch a glimpse of talents they might otherwise only have read about. When I saw them recently it was like watching a familiar film running through in slow motion. Perhaps I will look that way before long too.

PANCHO SEGURA

Pancho Segura turned professional very early in his career to play with Jack Kramer, Bobby Riggs and Danny Pails in America in 1948. This early baptism at the top world standard consolidated an already well developed game. He was a most unusual player to watch or play against. Like John Bromwich he had a two-handed shot on the right-hand side which became surely the best two-handed forehand ever seen. When he went to play a ball on his left-hand side he removed the left-hand but had to slide the right hand down to the end of the handle so that his backhand side was always weaker.

Pancho must be one of the most under-rated players of all time. Despite his small physique – he is no bigger than I am – he had a tremendous control on all his shots including his backhand and you never felt secure until you had actually won the point against him and heard the umpire say so. He possessed one of the greatest and shrewdest tennis brains I remember and could play any pattern of tennis on any surface. One of the great matches that stands out in my memory was the final of the Australian Professional Championships in 1953 against Frank Sedgman, who had recently turned pro. and was at his peak.

On fast grass Pancho moved the younger man all over the court and utterly bewildered him especially with the two-handed shot which he hit with such control that he could either pass or lob with the same action – something an opponent could not detect until it was too late. Sensibly he always tried to run around his weaker backhand to use this strong two-handed shot.

He came from Guyacil in Ecuador and had suffered from rickets as a boy which accounted for his bandy-legged gait which used to amuse spectators. His father had started him at the game very young, which is why he came to use two hands. Pancho was always one of the most popular players on our professional tours, on or off the court, and his failure to win any of the major championships, like Pancho Gonzales, stems from his early decision to turn professional.

He has become one of the shrewdest coaches in the game and his club in Los Angeles is a mecca for aspiring young players of all nationalities. Perhaps his greatest success has been with Jimmy Connors whom he has helped since Jimmy moved to the West coast from his home in Belleville, Illinois, in 1968 at the age of 16.

Truly Pancho Segura, who used to urge himself on during a match and now does the same for his charges, has been, and still is, one of the game's greatest characters.

TONY TRABERT

Tony was one of those typically aggressive American players whose record was quite outstanding. He was twice champion of his own country in 1953 and 55, twice French Champion in 1954 and 55 and Wimbledon

Tony Trabert, the all-American-boy who had an outstanding Davis Cup record with 27 wins from 35 singles between 1951 and 1955.

Champion in 1955. Had he won the singles in Australia that last year then he would have equalled Don Budge's Grand Slam before Rod Laver did so in 1962. Although he and Vic Seixas succeeded in winning the doubles there following their successful Davis Cup victory match against us at the end of December, in the singles he fell to Lew in the heat of Adelaide. Above all Trabert will be remembered as a great competitor who was relentless when ahead and courageous when behind. His Davis Cup single with Hoad in 1953 will be remembered by all who saw it and although he lost in five gruelling sets, his remark afterwards at the microphone, 'This will be remembered as Hoad's year. I promise you next year it will be Trabert's year' was prophetic for his 1954 Davis Cup form was outstanding, Trabert's great strength was his backhand which he hit with the thumb almost straight down the handle and took early with lift. He was a great athlete and a superb mover despite his size so that he often got to balls that appeared to be past him. He was one of the stalwarts of the professional tours in the late 1950s and came out of retirement to act as referee for the first two WCT finals in Dallas.

In selecting this list of some of my most prominent adversaries during the past 25 years I have omitted many fine players, but there has to be a limit. I could have talked for hours about that wonderful American match player Vic Seixas, or the flying Dutchman, Tom Okker, or the iron man from Prague, Jan Kodes. Then there are those two gifted left-handers, Tony Roche, now happily restored to fitness following years of nagging worry about his playing arm, and the graceful Spaniard, Manuel Orantes, who has inherited the mantle of another great Spaniard, Manuel Santana. Nor have I been able to comment upon the dynamic qualities of the present world leader, Jimmy Connors, or his predecessors at the top of the American game Stan Smith and Arthur Ashe. And I would have enjoyed discussing the bewitching artistry of Rumania's Ilie Nastase and the ruthless efficiency of John Newcombe's powerful game.

But I can assure you that in playing and competing against these great players of the past and present I have learned an enormous amount myself, about the game and about human nature. I always think that tennis brings out both the best and the worst in people by exposing them to the awesome pressures of the match court, where they are under the spotlight of world publicity. By and large I believe that good triumphs, and can think of no better preparation for life than the self-knowledge that is gained from competition at this level.

14. THE ROAD AHEAD

For the past 23 years, I have spent a great deal of my life living out of a suitcase – a penalty which all international professional sportsmen must pay in quest of fame and fortune. The fact that for 19 of those years I have been married has added greatly to the problem of constant travel. If it had not been for my wife, Wilma's, patient acceptance of an inevitable situation that neither of us has really enjoyed, I could never have continued in the game for as long as I have. During the long, lonely weeks spent in overseas hotels the telephone has been our saviour and I would cheerfully swap my last year's earnings for the amount we have spent on phone calls these last 19 years.

Upon Wilma has fallen the chief burden of bringing up our two sons, Brett and Glen, who are teenagers now, and I shall always regret that I was not able to spend more time with them in those precious years of growing up.

Fortunately, during the last two or three years, things have been easier to organise and we have been together much more. Wilma and the boys joined me in 1974, for example, during part of the four months

With the family at Forest Hills in 1972 on one of our rare tennis journeys together.

I spent playing Team Tennis with the Pittsburg Triangles. We were given the use of a nice two-bedroomed house in a private road that was part of Chatham University, it was comfortable and quiet, and we did not see much of the girl students, even during term time.

Nearby, there were three Laycold tennis courts which we could use and we had an occasional family outing on them when the intense Team Tennis playing schedule allowed. I also found time for the odd round of golf with Brett, a game which we both enjoy.

On one of those rare days off we organised a game of softball for all the members of the Triangles team – including Evonne Goolagong, Gerald Battrick, and Vitas Gerulaitis. My two boys joined in, and enjoyed dressing up in all the protective kit and uniforms which we borrowed from the University. There were lots of home runs and plenty of laughter – just the sort of break we all needed from the constant practice and busy travel schedules of Team Tennis.

I am often asked what I think of Team Tennis and I have to admit to conflicting emotions about the whole thing. At its best I could see that it appealed to the American sporting public, who are bred on inter-city rivalries in professional American sports like football, baseball, basketball, and ice hockey, rather like the intense inter-city feeling surrounding the British soccer leagues. But the problem of transforming what is after all really an individual sport into a team context is something which has not yet been satisfactorily solved.

Certainly our early decision to change the playing programme so that it included one set each of men's singles, women's singles, men's doubles, women's doubles, and mixed doubles helped matters. Matches were decided by the greatest number of games won when the results of all the sets were added together so that the final outcome often turned on the final set of mixed doubles. This set often became very exciting, as indeed the Wimbledon mixed doubles final so often does. All too few of them, however, depended on the outcome of the mixed. Because the earlier men's singles and doubles matches were often close, with strong servers holding their services easily on the fast Sportface carpet court that was used throughout the competition, the women's matches assumed a disproportionate importance. It was easier for a woman to have a decisive runaway victory than for a man, and accordingly the teams with a good women's singles player and a good women's doubles pair were the successful ones – the Philadelphia Freedoms with Billy-Jean King and Julie Anthony, the Minnesota Buckskins with Ann Jones, Mona Schallau, and Wendy Turnbull, and the Denver Racquets with Francoise Durr and Kristy Kemmer. We were very fortunate to have Evonne Goolagong and Peggy Michael who filled their roles in singles and doubles magnificently. Also, my task as player-coach was made much easier by the presence of Evonne's manager and guardian, Vic Edwards. He was a tower of strength in taking care of the countless details of planning and organisation associated with the running of a team.

The matches themselves were quite unlike any other sort of tennis I have ever played. From the outset the aim had been to attract a new non-tennis audience and, in a modest way, this objective was achieved. Total involvement was the theme and the new spectators were encouraged to root for their teams and hurl abuse at the enemy. The girls particularly found it very hard to concentrate through the personal remarks that were shouted at them.

It would not have been so bad if the ill-treatment had been restricted to away matches in strange cities – in many ways one could almost have enjoyed it as part of the legalised warfare that the promoters of Team Tennis wanted to create. But when home crowds started hounding their own players who were playing badly it was more than some of them could take. Evonne was near to tears on several occasions and the volatile Bob Hewitt was brought to boiling point on numerous occasions. His team, the Minnesota Buckskins, went bankrupt shortly before the end of the season and their supporters were among the most vociferous in the League. If Bob was playing well he was a hero – 'Hewitt can do it! Hewitt can do it!', they would chant. But woe betide him if he started to play badly. Then they would yell, 'Hewitt blew it! Hewitt blew it!' as the prospects of winning the match disappeared.

Our owner was Frank Fuhrer who, after the League's first year of financial failure, became its President for a short while before handing over to Larry King, Billy-Jean's lawyer/husband. Frank was one of the most dynamic and enthusiastic tennis buffs I've ever met but, as with some of the other owners, there was a lack of deep knowledge about the finer aspects of the game that sometimes made communication difficult. Nor did he thoroughly understand the way a player's mind works, so that all of us at times became involved in senseless arguments with him about what action we should take to improve our performances. After my experiences at Pittsburg I can understand why there is such a rapid turnover of football managers in British soccer.

One of the problems I faced in Pittsburg was a recurrence of the hay fever attacks which have often plagued me on visits to the grass court tournaments in Australia and Wimbledon. I well remember losing to Bob Lutz there in 1969, which was before I discovered the value of injections to counter the effects of this irritating allergy. They have helped tremendously in the last few years, and while in Pittsburgh I again went

My three most loyal fans (and sternest critics) sitting in the front row of Wimbledon's visitors box during the 1974 Final.

through the familiar tests where samples of various types of pollens and dusts are tried out on the arm before deciding what injections should be given.

My reasons for not returning to Team Tennis in 1975 (if, indeed, the League is still in business then) are largely family ones. I want to be around more at a time when the boys are entering an important stage of their education, so I shall be travelling and competing less. This will give me an opportunity to expand my coaching activities both in Australia and overseas. I shall be increasing my appearances for the BP International Tennis Fellowship at home and in Europe, doing similar work for my old friend, John Gardiner, at his beautiful tennis ranches in America, and I shall be starting a clinic programme for Cathay Pacific Airways in the Far East during the latter part of the year. This will still allow me to compete in six or seven tournaments each year at convenient moments without sacrificing my family. After such a full and rewarding life in tennis, this is the least I can do to show my gratitude for their patience with my competitive instincts.